Filling the Void

Filling the Void

Emotion, Capitalism and Social Media

Marcus Gilroy-Ware

Published by Repeater Books
An imprint of Watkins Media Ltd

19-21 Cecil Court
London
WC2N 4EZ
UK
www.repeaterbooks.com
A Repeater Books paperback original 2017
5
Printed and Bound in the UK by 4edge Limited
Distributed in the United States by Random House, Inc., New York.

Marcus Gilroy-Ware asserts the moral right to be identified as the author of this work.
For more information, see http://fillingthevoid.wtf

Cover design: Marcus Gilroy-Ware
Typography and typesetting: JCS Publishing Services Ltd, jcs-publishing.co.uk
Typeface: Minion Pro

ISBN: 978-1-910924-94-5
Ebook ISBN: 978-1-910924-85-3

To the lasting future of Planet Earth

Contents

Preface

Such is the astonishing overuse of low-paid casualised labour in UK universities that in April 2008, aged just 24, I was given the opportunity to teach master's students in one of the UK's most prestigious journalism departments, despite not having a master's degree or any qualification in journalism, and having never worked as a journalist. Especially given the difficult things it gave me to think about, this is an opportunity for which I will nonetheless be forever grateful. In my under-qualified, youthful foolishness, I was thrilled with the flattering "visiting lecturer" business card, not realising the scale of the challenge I had accepted. My responsibility was to teach these students about "online journalism," and the first task that this involved was to reverse engineer what good "online journalism" actually consisted of, so that my teaching of it would keep my passionate but demanding students happy.

I had been largely unaware of journalism's existential crisis, particularly in relation to the internet, but it didn't take long to figure out something was wrong. Already having a firm understanding of the web from a technical and a design perspective, my attentions focused on what journalism really and truly *meant* in an ontological sense, how that could look when expressed on the web, and what other people were doing in this area. As I explored the world of journalism beyond my department I found to my dismay that, where technology was not, at one extreme, being completely fetishised in the newsroom and was not, at the other extreme, inspiring utter fear amongst a technophobic old-guard, the emphasis was on the reproduction of existing journalistic practices in as faithful a way as the HTML medium would allow. Journalists, some of whose achievements in their own industry I respected enormously, seemed to think that they could start dictating the rules of this medium. As a digital native who had already been a keen web user for over a decade, I knew that this naïve, arrogant positivism about what they had always done would not fly, and that fetishising the technology would be no good either. Didn't they realise that this isn't how the web works? The web, I felt, had a culture, a way of working, and if journalists wanted to continue doing what was essential to their work — bringing people important information — they needed to pay attention to the ways in which the web functioned.

In the subsequent years, I disavowed myself of the idea that the web had a culture. Instead it seemed more likely that it was reflecting the culture of the moment in concentrated and variously distorted ways, like an old mirror. As the web quickly developed and became more and more integrated into people's lives, I became increasingly sure of one thing: Besides the "information super-highway" (more of an "information lane" these days), it is the non-factual, non-informational uses of the web that would come to dominate. Those in the business of communicating "facts" for a living would need to pay very close attention, and consequently, so did I.

In the course of this enquiry, I have become fascinated with one question: If people don't primarily use the web for information anymore, what do they mostly use it for, and why? What started with an interest in helping my students understand the flow of information over the web became a preoccupation with the use of networked media to learn something about people and society more generally. This runs somewhat against the tide of a significant proportion of research on social media, which has used behaviour to understand technology, instead of the reverse. Rather than just talking about journalism, we therefore needed to talk about the world in which journalism was trying to survive. To explain the true challenge facing my journalism master's students, I consequently found myself drawing on an increasingly broad array of materials. The works of people as diverse as Benedict Anderson, Harry Braverman, John Berger, Natalie Fenton, David Harvey, Julie E. Cohen, Evgeny Morozov, Rebecca Mackinnon, Mary Poovey, and Lawrence Lessig often became our readings or informed my lectures, and incidentally it is in the same spirit of incorporating any interesting or relevant material, regardless of intellectual tradition, that I have written this book.

In my first few years of teaching, the journalism department in that particular institution was mostly preoccupied with reproducing the golden era of journalism. While I enjoyed some good conversations, other colleagues showed the same impatience, contempt, and desire to oversimplify that often colours the demeanour of journalists confronted with "theory." Single-minded emphasis on graduates securing jobs within a shrinking journalism industry, drowning in its own dogma, did not help. If anybody had actually asked what I was teaching, they might well have been horrified by the outward-looking unorthodoxy, but for the most part I was sheltered by indifference. While I am pleased to say that this picture has much improved today as that department has become more well-rounded and forward looking, the enquiry that has followed that initial challenge has nevertheless been largely a conversation with academic colleagues from other disciplines, with friends and family, and with my students, who were far more open-minded, and many of whom became friends. In the end this was just as well, because the answers ultimately have only an indirect connection to journalism, even if they are directly applicable. Online media are the water in which journalists must swim; the party at which they must ingratiate themselves; the language in which they must gain fluency.

This book is the result of my explorations of our relationship to online media, and articulates the conclusions I have come to about human subjectivity, capitalism, and technology. I have made a series of arguments that combine the psychological and political, the philosophical and sociological. The arguments I present here will not accord with a conventional deterministic view of what social media "are doing to us," or to our culture, politics, friendships, etc. Nor will they accord with more nuanced critiques advanced in the past about identity, mass self-communication, new public spheres, subcultures, and so forth.

As the architecture and features of the web have developed, it has become increasingly clear that so-called "social media" are the means by which access to information and other content is facilitated online. Social media, while often subjected to facile, deterministic analysis, are a fascinating and varied site at which to observe culture, psychology, politics, language, emotion, and abundant human creativity, and information still has an important role to play on them too. At the same time, there are worrying aspects to how they are used. The compulsive, highly dependent relationship that many people have developed with social media, while it must not be judged or sneered at, needs to be understood widely in order to be ameliorated. What this usage says about our states of mind and the state of our societies is not a lesson about technology so much as about society and human subjectivity themselves. The ways that our vulnerability in relation to these media is being taken advantage of by large, cynical corporations are also worrying. Again, these are more lessons about capitalism's role in that society, rather than about technology. Similarly, whilst at times it will be necessary to give an account of the usage of social media and talk about *how* they are used, this is largely a book about *why* we use social media — a far more important question.

The five chapters of this book are a series of connected essays intended to provide a clear path through these questions, and the implications of their answers. Chapter One acts as an introduction and illustrates the breadth of this challenge in detail. It begins the process of making connections between how social media are used and the broader culture in which this often compulsive and self-detrimental usage takes place. Chapter Two looks in more detail at why so many people use social media, and what makes social media so hard to resist. It argues that we should see social media use as a form of hedonic media consumption, to which reward-seeking models of human behaviour can be applied, as with drugs or junk food. It explains how our relationship to social media is, much like these other forms of consumption, an attempt to compensate for poor emotional wellbeing. Chapter Three deals with the political and economic culture in which this compensation takes place — what are we compensating for when we use social media? What is making us unhappy? It was in a discussion of these questions that my friend Emanuelle Degli Esposti and I arrived at the idea of "filling" a "void." Chapter Four focuses attention on the companies that develop and own social media platforms, and explores their business models and the trends in capitalism that they embody. It argues that social media platforms exploit our compulsive, emotionally-driven relationship to them, seeking surplus value in the misery that capitalism itself creates. Chapter Five returns to the problems raised above: If the primary role of digital content and internet-based media is a compensatory emotional one in which information is secondary at best, and the forms of capitalism apparent in social media need to make no serious investment in the cultural norms, veracity or democratic role of their content, what are the implications for our cultures and public sphere more generally of social media usage on such a large scale?

When taken together, it is my humblest hope that the arguments in these chapters provide a useful, clear perspective on what is really going on in our use of social media.

Marcus Gilroy-Ware
Planet Earth, November 2016

— ONE —

Towards a holistic enquiry into social media

> That this technological order also involves a political and intellectual coordination may be a regrettable and yet promising development.
>
> Herbert Marcuse, One-Dimensional Man

One morning at the end of June 2015, having finally managed to make it to a decent beach for the first time in several years, I saw a young woman taking pictures of herself in her swimming costume with her iPhone, standing half-submerged in the water. Aware of the harsh critiques of young women's choices around how they represent themselves visually, and how the omnipotence of the smartphone camera has revealed new issues within that debate, I looked on and wondered what this young woman's own opinion of those issues would be. Was she taking control of her own representation, objectifying herself, or just having a nice time? Now didn't seem like the time to ask, and nor was I sure enough of my broken Italian. While I was struck by the intense concentration with which she posed for shot after shot, indifferent to the other people on the beach bearing witness to her digital self-portraiture, as a smartphone user myself I found the seeming nonchalance with which the device was handled in such close proximity to the water far more alarming. I didn't realise you could do that! Still unaccustomed to how beach culture had evolved to include smartphones, I quietly hoped her phone was insured for water damage and went back to my reading, realising I was the odd one out.

As innocent as a few self-portraits or "selfies" gleefully taken on a beach during a hard-earned holiday might seem, some people take far greater risks than having to lie to an insurance company in order to get their phone replaced because they accidentally dropped it in the Mediterranean trying to get that perfect shot. That same year, 2015, more than thirty people died around the world in various predicaments while trying to take selfies. In 2016, it only took until the end of June to reach the same number. Many of the people who have been killed taking selfies have been in the developing world, where the culture of "risk" avoidance has developed less quickly than the culture of smartphone usage, and access to dangerous but impressive selfie-taking areas such as railway tracks, the habitats of unpredictable wildlife, and tall, climbable structures is less restricted. Whether it is up to your waist in sea water or with an oncoming train visibly speeding towards you, the juxtaposition of the person taking the selfie with an exotic, unusual, or far-fetched background is exactly what makes the shot worthwhile and gives it its meaning. Impending danger in the background is only one type of emotional context in which to take a selfie. Other emotionally salient contexts are also common. Numerous teenagers have been criticised in the press for taking selfies at sombre sites such as the Auschwitz concentration camp in Poland or the memorial at the site of the Twin Towers in Manhattan. So many people have taken selfies at funerals, for example, that for a while there was an entire blog devoted to capturing them. When the blog's editors decided to cease posting in December 2013, their final post featured former US president Barack Obama taking a selfie with Danish prime minister Helle Thorning-Schmidt and British prime minister David Cameron at Nelson Mandela's memorial ceremony at the Soccer City stadium in Johannesburg. Former US president George W. Bush also took a selfie with U2 singer Bono at the same event. That same week, thousands of miles away, a tourist in Brooklyn, New York was widely criticised for taking a selfie as a man was attempting to throw himself off the Brooklyn Bridge in the background. Having been watching the unfolding situation for a few moments, she reportedly then photographed herself as officials attempted to talk the man down to safety behind her — successfully in the end. In September 2014 in Ankara, Turkey, a police official took a selfie showing in the background another desperate man moments from leaping to his death from a suspension bridge. The fact that such cases have tended to receive public outcry shows that we have not shaken a sense that some things perhaps shouldn't be recorded in this way, yet they continually happen anyway, which suggests a degree of tension or ambivalence about such actions. There is almost something desperate about our desire to perform online. In April 2016, when mentally ill man Seif El Din Mustafa hijacked a Cairo-bound flight and diverted it to Cyprus, passenger Ben Innes approached the hijacker to take a selfie with him, subsequently sharing the bizarre image online to great acclaim. That Innes was a health-and-safety auditor whose job was presumably to point out risk in exchange for money only makes the story more hilarious and bizarre. The desire to use images of yourself in unusual or salient contexts can even get you arrested. In 2016, domestic violence fugitive Mack Yearwood was so pleased to have been named "Wanted of the Week" by the police department in the town of Stuart, Florida, that he posted a copy of the genuine "wanted" poster as his own Facebook profile picture, eventually leading to his arrest. Even if not a "selfie" as such, it is instructive to note just how strong the desire to share images of ourselves that will somehow impress or shock can be.

As authoritative selfie-taking expert Kim Kardashian, author of *Selfish* (a coffee-table "book" consisting only of her selfies), once said: "I think it really takes about 15-20 selfies that someone takes on their phone before they post the right one." Similar to the numerous films in which a character holds up a recent daily newspaper to show that they are still alive, showing yourself in a given visual context is a way of emphasising your connection to a particular moment. Breanna Mitchell, one of the people shamed for taking a selfie at Auschwitz, told the press that she had shared the image in memory of her late father, who had had a love of history. You may be seeking validation, showing unity, making an homage, or it may simply be "cool," but these different purposes all have in common that they make your appearance in that location at that time into something performative. The fact that people are willing to go to such lengths to get the "right one" tells us that their motivations must be strong enough to challenge the normal reservations over decency or taste, or safety for that matter. Facing possible death on a train track, being at Nelson Mandela's memorial ceremony next to Barack Obama, looking "fly" in your swimwear on a beautiful Italian beach, or having a quiet but nonetheless highly public moment of "homage" at a former concentration camp all confirm this in different ways.

One can't necessarily assume that all of these images are intended to be uploaded to social media or shared publicly, of course, and in some cases the capturing of such images may well have been for strictly private record, as Thorning-Schmidt's selfie at Mandela's funeral with Cameron and Obama — which never surfaced — seems to have been. The data suggest, however, that most selfies are for sharing with a wider group of people via the internet, like George W. Bush's selfie with Bono at the same event, which was posted to image-sharing platform Instagram. Over three hundred million photos are uploaded to Facebook every day, and 95% of young adults admit to having taken at least one such picture of themselves. It is even possible to take animated selfies, which have become a regular feature of media-sharing app Snapchat.

A bit like how *Gulliver's Travels* is often abridged for children to only include his visit to Lilliput, the story of a selfie's appearance on a social network is just one small event in a longer story, which doesn't start with the snapping of the picture or stop at the successful distribution of the image to its intended audience. The full story highlights some of the broader issues with social media, and to illustrate this, we can take the posting of a selfie from the beach mentioned in the first paragraph of this chapter and fictionalise based on real-life data to show where the story might go next.

Let's say some hours after posting your selfie, you can't sleep. You check your phone again and it's 4am — the bright bluish screen of the device illuminating your face in an otherwise dark room. Not knowing what else to do with yourself and feeling that immediate sleep is unlikely, you open the Facebook app out of habit. How many more "likes" has the latest photo you just posted received? Has it reached a hundred yet? Why not? Has your current partner, who may be soundly asleep beside you, "liked" it yet? Why not? Did s/he really not like it? Is it because you might have put on weight, or are starting to get crow's feet? Perhaps you could never ask him/her directly, but you may very likely have wondered such things. We can go further still: Perhaps somewhere far away in another time zone, an old friend, who is suffering from depression, sees the photo in her news feed as she logs onto her Facebook for the fourth time in twenty minutes, looking for... she doesn't really know what. As she closes the web browser to end her Facebook session, the social network has not given her whatever she was looking for, and she feels more despondent and empty than ever. Elsewhere, a worker in the Philippines, hired by a firm subcontracted by Facebook Inc., has also seen the picture as part of a review process to make sure it conformed with the social network's "community standards." These workers are sometimes paid as little as one dollar per hour — sadly not a fiction (Webster, 2012).

Later that summer, let us continue to imagine, Facebook launch an advertising campaign for their social network, using real photos shared to the site, licensed from their users' profiles, including the shot you uploaded. Your likeness appears alongside others on billboards in London, Paris, New York, São Paulo, Rome, and other world capitals. To complete the narrative and provide some pleasing circularity, a friend, recognising you in the ad, takes a picture of this ad, posts it on Facebook, and tags you in it. You might be outraged by the usage of your likeness in this way, but permission for this type of usage has been repeatedly if unwittingly assented to every time you use Facebook, since this is when you agree implicitly to their terms and conditions of usage, which include the granting of a worldwide, non-exclusive license to use any of your content for any purpose. According to Facebook's terms and conditions of usage, the only way you could have prevented this happening was to delete the precious selfie from Facebook. The story of a standard selfie, it would seem, is not a particularly happy one. When selfies are shared, they are published onto pre-existing networks that are controlled by powerful, distant entities, but which reproduce and interact with the dynamics of existing social relations so that you won't notice. Your selfies and other materials are stored in privately owned databases whose owners grant themselves permission to use them in whatever way they choose, including in advertising. Social media platforms will mix your selfie in with content from other users, and provide a quantitative measure for others to leave feedback on each item in real time in the form of "likes," "shares," or "retweets," simultaneously providing the platform's owners with valuable real-time metadata and content analysis on every image, link, movie, or other media item, and providing the user with instant validation (or not).

Beyond posting

As much as selfies have become the focus of adventurous social-science academics and sardonic newspaper columnists alike, posting content — including self-portraits — to social media platforms is actually of secondary importance when compared with the *consumptive* use of social networks; that is, the viewing of and interaction with media content posted by other users, and that is where the main focus of any analysis should lie. As many as 25% of users say that they never post any updates on Facebook, according to Pew Research Center. Similarly with Twitter, 40% of users log in but never tweet. These users are nonetheless active, and form part of the audience for whose benefit selfies, along with most other status updates, tweets, and other content, are posted. On average, iOS and Android smartphone users spend 17% of all their time on their phones in the Facebook app, and 14% in a web browser such as Chrome or Safari for *all other mobile web browsing.*

The effects of social media use are pretty wide-ranging, and study after study shows that our satisfaction with life, body security, social relationships, and overall psychological wellbeing are negatively affected by the consumptive use of social media platforms, and improve quickly when we stop using them. Scientific studies are of course only one form of "evidence," and are often too positivistic in how they handle (or ignore) social constructs, but they can still contribute a lot to a broader analysis without requiring that we embrace all their assumptions. A 2014 study found that increased time using Facebook's photos functionality specifically (as opposed to the platform's other functionalities) was correlated with increased body dissatisfaction and self-objectification in US teenage girls (Meier & Gray, 2014). A 2015 study found that following larger numbers of strangers on Instagram predicted increased depressive symptoms in young adults. Amongst those following the highest percentages of strangers, "more frequent Instagram use had direct associations with greater depressive symptoms" (Lup, Trub & Rosenthal, 2015). One survey found that as many as 66% of teenage girls using Facebook claim to have been bullied via the platform, 19% via Twitter, and 9% via Instagram (Steinmetz, 2014). Another study in 2009 found that Facebook "may be responsible for creating jealousy and suspicion in romantic relationships" (Muise, Christofides & Desmarais, 2009), and yet another found that "the longer people have used Facebook, the stronger was their belief that others were happier than themselves, and the less they agreed that life is fair" (Chou & Edge, 2012). Research has also shown that use of social media is likely to make you less happy generally, or in more scientific language, causes an acute decline in "subjective emotional wellbeing." A 2013 study of Facebook by Ethan Kross and colleagues, based mostly at the psychology department at the University of Michigan, is especially prominent in this research. Although the methodology of this study — texting people five times a day to ask them quantitative questions about where their emotions and social media use fall between one hundred, "a lot," and zero, "not at all" — leaves a lot to be desired, the results and analysis presented do show a significant causation: People go on Facebook, and subsequently feel emotionally worse as a result in the next two-to-three-hour period, and increasingly dissatisfied with their lives over the course of the two-week study. "Facebook use predicts declines in the two components of subjective wellbeing: how people feel moment to moment and how satisfied they are with their lives," the study says. "The more participants used Facebook, the more their life satisfaction levels declined over time" (Kross et al, 2013). More recently, a 2016 study by psychologists at the University of Pittsburgh School of Medicine similarly found that social media were "significantly associated with increased depression" (Lin et al, 2016). Without having spent the time trawling through cyberpsychology journals, many people will feel these effects, particularly in the case of emotions, without being fully aware of their causes and associated behaviours, but that is all the more reason to take such effects seriously, rather than discount them.

The effects of our consumption of social media are not only psychological either. We are also physiologically affected by social media, and especially the devices via which we access them. As of April 27th 2016, 54% of Facebook users use the platform only via a smartphone, and according to Buzzfeed's own industry insights (2014), US adults aged eighteen to thirty-four spend an average of five hours and twelve minutes per day on their smartphones. Many readers will at least be able to imagine checking their phones in the middle of the night as in our story above, and possibly entering the Facebook app or Twitter app, but these devices are far from salubrious. The compulsive checking of social media, email, or other media from a smartphone can interfere with our sleeping patterns if it occurs before or during sleep hours. Whether you are checking for likes on your Instagram selfie, witty Tweet, or sarcastic Facebook post, studies show that if you do this in the middle of the night or up to an hour before going to bed, your sleeping patterns can be significantly disrupted. One such study "indicates that during laboratory exposure to 884 MHz wireless signals, components of sleep believed to be important for recovery from daily wear and tear are adversely affected" (Arnetz et al, 2008). Other research suggests it is not only the electromagnetic waves from your smartphone that interfere with your sleep, but also the frequency of light emitted by the blue pixels that are part of the RGB screen, so much so that "an average person reading on a tablet for a couple hours before bed may find that their sleep is delayed by about an hour" (Holzman, 2010). In version 9.3 of their mobile operating system iOS, Apple even introduced a feature to mitigate this effect by making the screen of your device glow more towards the orange part of the spectrum. The show must go on, after all!

Beyond disrupting our sleep, there are also other physical dangers. A study commissioned by US mobile carrier AT&T found that seven in ten people use their smartphone while driving, with four in ten admitting to using social media while at the wheel. One in ten even use video chat *while driving* (!). For a country with approximately 250 million cars on the road and a driving age as low as fourteen in some states, that is a hugely worrying statistic, but perhaps says more than any other about how desperate people seem to be to continue using social media. There is an awful lot invested in social media maintaining their perception as innocent, fun, social, and above all, harmless. We shouldn't be so sure.

What we can be sure of is that our use of networked, consumer technology, and particularly the combination of smartphones and social networks, despite being rapidly and intimately incorporated into our lives on an unprecedented scale, is not particularly good for us in the long run. Being on social media in moderation and using smartphones to access them may be perfectly innocent in themselves, and many people still voluntarily use social media for basic, prosaic reasons, but there are aspects of what social media does to us individually, what it means for our societies, and what it can tell us about how we live that are troubling and that need to be articulated for all to hear. Our desperation to take dangerous selfies and compulsively check social media in the middle of the night in a way that disturbs our sleep, or while driving so that we end other people's lives and ruin our own, are just a few of the more colourful examples.

The big questions

I want to make it clear that I do not hate social media and I am not arguing that you should either. There are a lot more useful things to say about the world than dividing it into "good" and "bad." The idea for this book came partly from the ambivalence of my own relationship with social networks and apps, and when I finished the first draft of its manuscript, I shared this fact with some of my friends using a social network. The point of outlining how social media are not as good for us as they claim to be is not to be judgemental of their usage or dictate what people should or shouldn't do. We are "only human" after all, and human vulnerability and entrapment in habitual self-detriment should be met with compassion and solidarity. But just like those pet parrots that compulsively pluck out their own feathers, surely we cannot be content to simply look on without objectively wondering: Why? If it is so easy to demonstrate the downside of social media usage, why do so many people keep using it? It's not as if the pathologies described above pass unnoticed in the end.

Were the activity something else more stigmatised, such as alcohol, we would immediately respond to the scenario with a well-known label: Addiction. But addiction is a slippery diagnosis that tends to have lesser or greater applicability depending on the activity or substance to which it is applied, and there is not always a strict basis on which to decide when an individual is *addicted* and when their behaviour in relation to a given stimulus is simply excessive. While there is a tendency for the media to portray excessive social media usage as "addiction," it is more complicated than simply applying our understanding of addiction to a new area. Addiction, as psychologist Richard Wood (2007) points out, is a concept largely borrowed from the diagnosis of substance addiction in the American Psychological Association's *Diagnostic and Statistical Manual of Mental Disorders* (DSM), and so is a metaphorical rather than direct characterisation when applied to media usage such as video games or social media. That is not to say that one can only truly be addicted to substances — gambling addiction is a very real problem in some people's lives, and so is pornography addiction, but we would be better placed to learn from addictive patterns, rather than insisting on seeing them everywhere. True addiction, whether to substances or media, also has a number of hallmarks that aren't necessarily present in social media addiction. For a start, more of the same stimuli is needed over time because a tolerance develops, and users become desensitised to the stimuli that previously gave them what they wanted. Gamblers no longer feel the same rush when gambling the same sums, heroin users quickly develop a tolerance to the effects of the drug and require an increased amount to feel the same high, and pornography users often lose the ability to enjoy actual sexual contact, and have to seek out increasingly extreme materials just to get the same stimulation. Furthermore, addictions can usually develop to a point where the user has completely lost control of their life. Drug use, alcohol and gambling addiction are again the most common examples. Addictions also frequently lead to identifiable and dangerous withdrawal symptoms if the activity or behaviour to which the individual is addicted is taken away. While there is some indication that certain social media are as hard to give up as alcohol or nicotine (Hofman, Vohs & Baumeister, 2012) and social media-driven usage on a *smartphone* can cause withdrawal-like symptoms such as anxiety when unavailable (Moeller, Powers & Roberts, 2012), there is no evidence that these symptoms are medically serious in the same ways, for instance, as those of heroin withdrawal.

Many of us love to hate social media and roll our eyes if they are overemphasised. It's not uncommon to have at least one friend who has left Facebook, their name greyed out and their previous comments and interactions all gone without trace. But despite such unease about the role of social media in our lives or in society in general, we continue to use them. Huge numbers of us use social media in ways that can demonstrably have subtly detrimental effects on us, for huge amounts of time, and many of us behave as if we are apparently desperate to continue doing so. There are now more Facebook users logging onto the site at least once a month — 1.79 billion at the time of writing — than there are Catholics, Muslims, or left-handed people in the world. Over a billion of these people check Facebook every day. In 2015 it was reported that the UK's Royal Navy was having difficulties recruiting because younger candidates couldn't face the idea of being trapped in a submarine underwater for up to 90 days, with no access to the web or social media. "The fact that you are disconnected from the world wide web and Twitter is actually a significant barrier to recruiting young people," defence consultant Nick Chaffey told the *Daily Mail* (2015). According to research agency We Are Social, the average UK social media user spends two hours and thirteen minutes on social media per day, while the global average for internet users isn't far behind at one hour and forty-nine minutes.

What do these people get from their use of Facebook, Twitter, Instagram, or any other "social media" platform that could possibly explain such an extreme relationship to them? These hordes of people must be driven toward these platforms by some fairly powerful forces, but what are they? And are these forces external to these people, acting upon them to motivate them onto these platforms, or do they come from within these people's own minds? These questions frame the need to build a much clearer picture of what is really going on. They are the kinds of questions it is essential to ask about any society in which large numbers of people do something that is arguably to their own detriment. To some extent, participating in things that we know cause harm is a common feature of life in contemporary consumerist culture, but this usually occurs in a context where people feel they have no choice. The emission of carbon dioxide into the atmosphere, for example, is something that is widely regarded to be bad for the environment, and for the people and wildlife that live on planet Earth, yet almost all of us who believe global warming is a problem are still complicit in making this situation worse because our need for energy or transportation (not to mention our hunger for steak, iPhones, and cheap consumables manufactured on the other side of the world) requires that carbon dioxide and methane be emitted. But technology isn't supposed to be the same, is it? Why on earth do so many people find social media so hard to put down?

Escaping rational positivism

In the past, when calling our motivations for using social media into question, I have been scolded by people who say things like: "But there are lots of benefits to social media. You can keep in touch with friends, or stay up to date with what is happening in the world." The liberal, market-oriented view of consumer technology has always focused on its positive aspects and encouraged us to believe that our relationship with technology is one that empowers us with new choices and sacred freedoms. Long before the age of apps, the "world wide web," upon which the original social media websites grew, was hailed as a practical advantage to its users; a growing series of tools to make life easier. We are now, you often hear, an "information society," largely thanks to the internet. Writing before "social media" existed, Todd Gitlin (2003) argued that terms such as "information society" or "information age" were "instant propaganda" for a positivist view of what the technology of the internet could bring its users. "Who in his right mind could be against information or want to be without it? Who wouldn't want to produce, consume, and accumulate more of this useful stuff, remove obstacles to its spread, invest in it, see better variants of it spring to life?" he asked rhetorically. After all, technology brings progress! A CompuServe ad from 1982 illustrates this well:

> Someday, in the comfort of your own home, you'll be able to shop and bank electronically, read instantly updated newswires, analyse the performance of a stock that interests you, send electronic mail across the country, then play bridge with three strangers in LA, Chicago and Dallas. *Welcome to Someday.*

Interestingly, Steve Jobs was still evangelising about essentially the same types of capabilities when the iPhone launched 25 years later in 2007, the only difference being that the "comfort" of one's "own home" was no longer a necessity for such affordances so much as a hindrance — classrooms, museums, public transport, or behind the wheel of a moving car have now all become common locations for the same activities to occur.

One can't sensibly disagree that social media, and the internet more generally, are capable of providing real practical benefits, and there is no denying that some of these benefits are indeed social in their nature, but this should not mean that social media are somehow immune from proper analysis or critique, or that their sole usage is that of basic practicality or sociality. Just as Frankfurt School philosophers Theodor Adorno and Max Horkheimer took issue with the positivism and rationalism of the enlightenment, we cannot allow any such pragmatic account of social media to be our prevailing analysis. A bit like saying "red wine helps you live longer," it ignores the moderation that is required, the dependency that can and often does form, the numerous other inevitable drawbacks, and the broader diagnosis as to why certain aspects of life might be amiss to start with. Just as nobody who drinks wine daily does so *primarily* for the health benefits without kidding themselves, nobody who uses social media in the compulsive and self-defeating ways that have become common does so purely for its social or practical benefits.

To say that social media and the internet are not predominantly practical is not, however, to say that they do not offer any practical benefit. Rather, the argument must be that such practical uses are not what drive their use. Briefly, it is worth exploring some of the areas where social media are used rationally or with a clear, conscious purpose.

News & information

The nomenclature of a "news feed" used on some social networks is curious given that such a proportion of the content it tends to contain is not "news" in any conventional sense. This emphasis owes more to the idealistic history of the web as an "information superhighway," but like the emphasis on sociality, it obfuscates the timeline's other more common, if dysfunctional, purposes. Social media are sometimes an important means of access to debate and to information, and a study by Pew Research Centre from May 2016 reported that 62% of

US adults get some of their news via social media, with 18% doing so "often". Since information can easily be found elsewhere however, the case for social media as an information-centric architecture is a weak one. As we will see in chapters Two and Five respectively, social media are often a far more important source of non-information and even *disinformation* than they are a bona-fide source of trusted information.

Fundraising and organising

Social media can be used effectively as a fundraising or awareness-raising tool. According to the *New Yorker*, the ALS "Ice Bucket Challenge" of 2014, although widely derided as a fad, was an indisputable success. Despite many copycat videos featuring people dumping ice cold water on themselves without raising any money for the cause at all, the 440 million videos, viewed 10 billion times in all, raised a staggering 220 million dollars globally for ALS organisations, with the American ALS Association receiving "thirteen times as much in contributions as what it had in the whole of the preceding year." Much as the videos may have become annoying after a while, the campaign was a uniquely social media-native affair and exemplifies the ways in which social media can concentrate the web's practicality and sociality to useful ends.

Romance

The benefits of social media can also be personal: According to a 2013 report from Pew Research Center, "One in ten Americans have used an online dating site or mobile dating app themselves, and many people now know someone else who uses online dating or who has found a spouse or long-term partner via online dating." Whether dating sites count as "social media" in the most common sense of the term is debatable, since one of the defining hallmarks of contemporary social media is that they are generalised, multi-purpose platforms (see Chapter Four for a discussion of this generality), whereas dating apps and websites are far more specific, but even away from purpose-driven dating apps and websites, people have always met on the web for sex, romance, and true love. In one recent example, couple Victoria Carlin and Jonathan O'Brien got married after Carlin tweeted in 2012, "Well I'm in love with whoever is manning the Waterstones Oxford Street account. Be still my actual beating heart." Four years later in July 2016, Carlin tweeted, "Dear reader, I married him #noreally #yeahidunnohoweither." Again, critiques of social media do not need to be blind to such stories; they are not counter-examples and they do not disprove anything that will be argued in this book. Rather, the very fact that this story and a few others like it are reported in the press and capture people's imaginations is not only because they are saccharine or heart-warming, depending on how romantic you are, but because the chances of them happening are astronomical — such benefits are certainly not the reason people are constantly checking Facebook.

How social *are* "social media"?

Swiss semiotician Ferdinand de Saussure argued that, rather than things existing first and then being labelled by language, a word being used to denote something was an act of construction and that language was a way to confer socially constructed meaning onto the world. The term "social media" is a good example of this. It insists that social media primarily facilitate our social lives. While no doubt lexically sound to begin with, this signifier seems to imply that the capacity to be social, referred to by social scientists as "sociality," is the only attribute worth using as a descriptor, rather than an attribute that is arguably just a layer woven into its other functionalities to make them more appealing, and we are left with something of a misnomer. They could be called "sleep-disruptive media," or "depressive media," but then Facebook's shareholders might not be so happy. "Social media" is not a neutral term, and should not be above critique. What could be wrong with "media" that are "social"? It's like calling them "fun media" or "friends media." This characterisation is a huge part of how the internet's positive side and capabilities have been sold to us, and has even shaped much of the research into the role that social networks play (e.g. Nadkarni & Hofmann, 2012). Most major technological introductions are accompanied by highly positive or utopian thinking, and the web was no exception. While sociality may have been redemptive of an earlier, more boring web, today it obfuscates the other roles that "social" media have come to have, explored in the remaining chapters of this book.

Sociality can rarely occur without denoted spaces, be they rooms in a house, or buildings and spaces within a city. The perception of the early web as a *separate space* is an interesting part of its social history, and the idea of an exciting new "cyber" space was a part of how this utopianism was articulated. US internet lawyer Julie E. Cohen tells us, "The cyberspace utopians have been most influential [...] precisely where their contribution is least remarked: in catalysing the narrative construction of cyberspace as separate space" (2007). Sociality on the web proved most popular with people who were otherwise restricted in their sociality and social space: Teenagers, reclusive individuals, and enthusiasts in very specific niches who were not geographically close enough to one another to discuss their passions in "real" space. It was a trail that had been blazed long before it became mainstream with consumer networks such as America Online, or AOL. Forums, news groups, and bulletin boards, although seldom pitched as nominally social *for sociality's sake*, provided early forms of sociality by connecting people who wanted to discuss highly specialised interests with others who shared them.

They also involved features that survive to this day on social media platforms, such as discussion threads and emoticons. AOL was one major platform on which the web's early sociality gained commercial and social momentum, with teenagers and middle-schoolers tying up household phone lines for hours so that nobody else could use them, because to be online was a social activity rather than a purpose-oriented tool, yet did not require even leaving the house. AOL also foreshadowed many features of contemporary social networks with features such as user profile pages, screen names, avatars (profile pictures), and text-based real-time conversations. As we should be aware today too, teenagers are often early adopters in some ways because, as Sherry Turkle (2011) has written at length, they use technology to escape. It is when their parents start using the same technology that you know it has gone mainstream, at which point the teenagers will look for something else (Wiederhold, 2012), but the importance of social media for them as a primary social conduit cannot be underestimated. Data published in 2016 show that the widespread adoption of social media since 2007 has coincided with a 45% decline in teenage pregnancy over the same period (Bingham, 2016), so the illusion of the web as a space, albeit felt rather than stated outright, does at least have some advantages. For teenagers, recluses, and "geeks" alike, the sense of the web as a separate space into which you could escape was and remains an alluring one, even if the "cyberspace" terminology was not consistently an explicit part of the experience, and is now virtually unheard of.

For everybody else, for whom satisfactory sociality already existed, the internet was not initially an obviously social technology. Social media use as a normative, mainstream, grown-up activity did not begin until the social networks we use today, such as Facebook, appeared — more than fifteen years after the original web was introduced. If Facebook was the only way to be friends, the 76% of the globe's population not (yet?) on Facebook at the time of writing would have *no friends*. If Twitter was the only way for us to partake in social news consumption and information exchange, there would have been no such thing as a public sphere until 2006 when it was founded, and digital humanities colleagues wouldn't be quoting Habermas quite so reliably as they do. In other words, the sociality of "social media" is not an explanation in itself for why we use them so much because the things it is claimed they do for us socially are largely behaviours that predate their arrival by decades or even centuries, subject to a few enhancements. We should be very careful about confusing an explanation of why so many people use social media with an account of their practical or purely social — in the literal sense — affordances. The internet in general has provided a means to communicate in real time using text, sound, image, or video, with people in any part of the globe, often with no additional cost besides that of the device being used to connect and the internet connection itself. That is an amazing capability which some social networks have now incorporated. It might be what people use Facebook for sometimes, but it is not *why* people use *Facebook* specifically, to begin with.

Those who scolded me for seeming as though I had overlooked the social benefits they had experienced on social media were missing the point. It is not that "social media" aren't intensely social, so much as the fact that they neither have the exclusivity on sociality in the way that their name appears to suggest, nor function in an exclusively social role, as we will see in Chapter Two. Furthermore, as sociologist C. Clayton Childress (2012) has observed, *all media are social*, and to allow ourselves to believe that "social media" are uniquely so is shaky ground at best. He asks: "But if these new forms of media are social media, does this imply that older mediums such as film, television, and books are anti-social?" One of the most important things we do with any medium is to consume and share it *with others*. As an example of this, Childress uses the work of sociologist Elizabeth Long (1994), whose analysis of women and literature indirectly takes issue with the myth of un-social media, or "the reader who reads alone":

While we might imagine a solitary reader getting lost in a good story as she sits by her window, this picture masks the simple fact that the achievement of literacy is itself a complex and collective social accomplishment. [...] Perhaps most importantly for readers, the myth of the "reader who reads alone" masks the deep conversations that reading engenders; talking with others about books we have read is one of the many social pleasures of the medium.

As much as the long-term presence of the web in our lives has a history of being something useful and ultimately sociable, we are kidding ourselves if we think that such uses alone drive the popularity of social media in their current iteration. A better justification for the use of the word "social" would be as an acknowledgement that users' sociality has in some ways become a commodity, harvested by a social network's owners. While social networks obviously involve people who are known to you socially in some sense or other, the fact that they are called "social media" should not be seen as a reflection of what they offer their users, so much as what their users give to them.

A positivistic emphasis on the mechanical features and convenient affordances offered by social networks is both deterministic and naïve. Some uses for the internet, including aspects of social media, are useful, and some are social, but these aren't what make social media irresistible. It's time to talk about what does.

How social media are making us more technologically deterministic

I was once commissioned to write an article entitled "Is Social Media Making Us Lonely?" for a start-up technology publication (2013). In the course of researching this article, something dawned on me. It seemed like instead of social media making us lonely, loneliness was, if anything, making us turn to social media. The studies on this relationship are conflicting. In truth, it's a lot more of a cycle, and loneliness is far too specific of a condition since it is itself a symptom with an array of social causes (see Chapter Three). Nonetheless this raised the important issue of causality: When people consider a technology's role in their lives, they tend to think about how it has been or will be the *cause* of various changes in us and in the world. That is exactly what the editor and I had done in agreeing on an article with that headline, and we were not alone. Endless blog articles with titles like "How social media is changing the way we (do business/ make friends/have sex/do other everyday activity)" betray this logic and show it to be widespread. The BBC's World Service even bizarrely asked on its website: "Is social media fueling a craze for stronger [male] jaw lines?" (2016). Some academics and behavioural scientists are guilty too — one of the studies cited in this chapter begins its abstract with "The social network site Facebook is a rapidly expanding phenomenon that is changing the nature of social relationships," and many others do similarly. Social media can certainly affect us, but does our use of them really *make* us *do* anything? Social relationships are as old as humankind itself; after thousands of years of human genetic and social evolution, is it really Facebook — about twenty million lines of PHP code; a privately-owned Californian database with a website (and app) user interface — that is changing the very nature of social relationships, something so central to human essence? Unlikely, if you think about it a bit harder. Facebook isn't changing anything except its own features (as explored in Chapter Four); it's a combination of the people who created Facebook, the people who use it, their relationships and respective needs, of which the Facebook platform itself is only the mediator, and lastly the society in which this interaction takes place. The same goes for Twitter, Instagram, Weibo, VKontakte, LinkedIn, and all other social networks that people actually use (so, not Google Plus). Banal, throwaway statements of the form "social media is changing us" typify a variety of lazy thinking known as *technological determinism*, typical of how technologies are often discussed and understood as their usage changes gear from early adopters to more mainstream usage. To see things according to a technologically deterministic outlook is to believe that technology can somehow induce or suppress our behaviour, as though we have no control. Technological determinism is the belief that adding a "pride" flag emoji will make life substantially easier for LGBTQ individuals, or that replacing the "gun" emoji with a fun-looking bright-green water pistol will somehow do anything to ameliorate gun violence. If we think of technology as being external to our humanity or agency in this way, we easily forget that the people who designed and built that technology, unlike the technology itself, have intentionality and may well be interested in steering and controlling our behaviour. When it is put like this, the complete loss of agency on our behalf that it implies becomes clear, and its absurdity is revealed. In the first instance, your brain is what determines your behaviour and responds to your environment, not some "brogrammers" at Facebook or Snapchat. The technology invites you do certain things in ways that are undoubtedly influential, but there is nothing in that technology that forces you to do them.

Another problem with technological determinism is that the opportunity to identify the real cause of our own behaviours is often lost. Rather than speculating about what it is that technology *makes* us feel or do, we would do well to start asking what it is in us that makes us find any given technology — or action within that technology, such as "liking" something — appealing. Technology allows, more than it causes, and if our behaviour changes when a new technology comes along it is because we are finally able to do something that we already had a propensity to do. When a technology becomes as general as social media has done, this is a difficult question, but all the more necessary.

Where technological determinism is one extreme because it externalises our behaviours onto a technology and eliminates our capacity to think and act for ourselves, the other extreme is also problematic. In most societies, there is generally a tendency to pathologise, medicalise, and even penalise individuals for behaviours deemed undesirable or deviant, without looking at any of the broader societal factors that may have led to those behaviours. Broader debates do happen on occasion, but they seldom receive much attention or credibility, and both conservative and liberal politics tend to favour total individual responsibility so that questions about underlying systemic causes need not be asked. If people riot, they're "animals"; if somebody carries out a mass shooting, they're either "crazy" or it's because of their fanatic religiosity (depending on the religion).

Individual responsibility is the sacred preserve of modern economics, justice, and ethics, yet there is every reason to believe that when a society is less happy, more repressed, pressurised, or unbalanced, people are more likely to seek out pleasure and comfort, and the dysfunctional behaviour of its members in order to do so will begin to increase. If your "friend" Johnny spends an excessive amount of time on Facebook, for example, is it because Johnny is at fault, or because Johnny's brain, being that of a human being, will tend to seek certain things that Facebook convincingly promises, and because the economic and social pressures under which Johnny and many people in Johnny's society live are inclined to exacerbate compulsive behaviours such as the overuse of social media?

The tendency when addressing social media is to normalise their scale and presence in our lives, but like Marx's idea of the *superstructure*, consumer technology often reflects, echoes, and subtly reinforces the prevailing norms and assumptions of the culture that gave rise to it, and the lowercase-p politics that can be identified in that culture. Rather than determining culture, *technology is culture*, and it is essential to start seeing it as such. In an age where technologies such as Facebook are so much a part of the broader culture, this inevitably means that there is a contradiction between technological determinism and individual responsibility; you cannot have a situation in which technology can and does *make* us do things, but capitalism, austerity, inequality, and injustice — all also cultural and historically produced — cannot and do not. Either culture affects our behaviour or it doesn't.

The only resolution to this contradiction has been to imagine that technology is somehow outside of, and deterministic of, culture. A far better basis on which to try and seek answers, however, is to say that it is our cultural and economic environment, in combination with our brains, that *makes* us do things, and interaction with the technology that that environment produces is just one of several means by which this happens. When such connections are revealed, and technology is shown to be intimately connected with the culture, economy, and psychology of everyday life in a given period of history, it becomes a useful gauge by which we can ascertain the health of our democracy, culture, and collective consciousness, and social media are an especially good opportunity for an accurate reading of those cultures and economies. Those seeking to understand social media as a technology can learn a great deal from looking at the culture that produced them and drives their usage; those looking to learn about that culture can do so partly from examining its technologies.

This anti-deterministic way of looking at things also reminds us that accepting social media as a normative part of human life is a choice that we don't have to make, just as not all of us like dubstep, BBQ ribs, or *Sex and the City*. However, identifying social media as a subjective feature of our cultural landscape does not mean that we can take our eyes off it. Even if we have decided to abstain, or never chose to participate in "that Twitter thing" in the first place, we still urgently need to consider digital technology's place in our lives, however distant we think we can be from it. It is in our lives whether we like it or not by virtue of being part of the lives of those around us. According to Pew Research Center, half of US adults who are not on Facebook live with somebody who is, and there are also increasing uses of social media as a privatised extension of public

Traffic sign, Euston Rd, London

life; local governments, police, and municipal authorities now often use Twitter to broadcast important infrastructural information, for example.

This only confirms what we already know: Those who are not interested in international affairs are still affected by war; those who can see nothing of interest in economics are still impacted by currencies, markets, and reckless lending; and those who know nothing about the law are still bound and prosecuted by it. Even if you aren't given to such trivialities as social media at all, consider yourself well above posting a selfie, never check your Facebook or Twitter from your phone — let alone in the middle of the night or while driving — or aren't on any social networks at all, it is in all of our interests to pay attention.

It is therefore time to take a wide-ranging look at how our changing relationship with technology and networks originates from broader cultural, political, and economic questions about the lives we lead; a holistic, general, critical account of social media, not as a "separate space," as past analyses have characterised the web, but as a digitally arranged, tightly integrated extension of the very same cultures, economies, and social relations that we already inhabit. A bit like an ocean's currents, there are underlying patterns and tendencies in our usage of social media that do not originate in them, but in ourselves and the societies we create, and as social networks encircle more and more of our digital activity and daily life, we will come to see that there is an awful lot at stake. This is the kind of analysis that will be attempted in the chapters that follow. While this book may well be pigeon-holed as a book about social media, it is not a book about Facebook or Twitter or any other specific platform *per se*, and should not be taken as a specific analysis of certain platforms or websites. It is a book about human subjectivity, capitalism, its culture, and the effects and consequences of the combinations these produce. Since we can read Facebook, Twitter, and others as cases of a broader phenomenon that can and likely will be reproduced and amended by other corporations in the future, the ins and outs of *specific* platforms like Facebook or Twitter or the companies that happen to build, run, and own these platforms are relevant only insofar as they illustrate manifestations of a broader, underlying pattern.

We cannot allow the character or narrative of our relationship to social media to be dictated by the forces of capital that own and benefit from these platforms, since no motivation would exist to exercise the necessary degree of scrutiny towards Facebook, Twitter, and other such enterprises. If the companies of the same names are asked about the effects their products may have on their users, they will make an unqualified and positive assessment of their own products and deny that there is anything detrimental about their platforms if they are used properly, or that they are responsible for their misuse. But as we will see in Chapter Four, your activity on so-called "social media" can create enormous revenues for these platforms' parent companies.

These corporations' very existence, not to mention quarterly profits, are dependent on our continuing usage. The answers must therefore come from those who have nothing to gain from the economic success of social media. There may be no more radical or important act in our time than to draw attention to the connections that entrenched, powerful institutions wish to remain out of sight. These connections are hiding in plain sight, however, and where this work may not always offer solutions to the — at times — alarming pictures it will paint, it is hoped that the articulation of these connections with sufficient care will itself be a useful and constructive contribution to our understanding. What is attempted here is therefore a radical exercise of "connecting the dots," such that, with enough work, a picture begins to appear that shows social media users their true relationship with social media, and shows us our true relationship with capitalism.

The same picture is probably very clear to the large corporations that give us social media platforms. Inside Facebook, Twitter, Google, and other smaller enterprises involved in bringing social media platforms to market, the connections between culture, capital, and psychology that will be revealed in this work are already well understood. But where such connections are a *strategy* for these organisations, understanding them is for us a way not to be outwitted; a way for us to be aware of our own position within that picture. While the connections made in this work are the stuff of important meetings at Facebook, the stakes for us are much higher.

It is my hope in writing this book that readers will be provided with a map for situating themselves in relation to technology, to social media, and to capitalist culture. Especially for those who intend to continue using social media, it is essential to understand the relationship between all three and to derive from that a clearer idea of what you are really doing, and who you are really serving, when for example you check your Facebook at night or tweet a selfie.

— TWO —

The empty fridge

Social media as consumption, pleasure, and emotion regulation

He that loves pleasure must for pleasure fall.

Christopher Marlowe, *Doctor Faustus*

Many of us pursue pleasure with such breathless haste that we hurry past it.

Søren Kierkegaard

There are only two professions that call the people who use their products "users." One is drug dealers, the other is us [software developers/designers].

Aral Balkan

I've learned that people will forget what you said, people will forget what you did, but people will never forget how you made them feel.

Maya Angelou

The last chapter asked an important question: If social media are not good for us, aren't uniquely social, and don't on the whole make us feel better about our lives (let alone our bodies), why do we find it so hard to avoid using them? This and the next chapter will endeavour to provide the answers. When Kari J. Milberg crashed her car in 2013, tragically killing her daughter and two nieces, it was because she was attempting to use Facebook on her smartphone *whilst driving*. Any argument that social media usage is primarily driven by basic practical and social motivations such as keeping in touch with friends and staying informed simply fails to explain the pattern of compulsive usage behaviours such as Milberg's. The irrationality with which people are increasingly using social media suggests that they are driven by far deeper and more powerful psychological forces that social media platforms are able to unleash and harness. The first aspect of social media that needs to be interrogated is therefore the individual, subjective experience of using social media and the psychological drives within us that social media exploit, whether by design or otherwise.

Human beings, whether we like it or not, aren't always very sensible. This is not intended as a value judgement — lots of things need not be "sensible," or are conducted harmlessly without "sense" ever being involved: Smelling a rose as you walk past on a mid-summer's day is not "sensible," for example. Neither is writing poetry, playing basketball, or listening to an electric bass solo, but all are of unquestionable value. People who focus too much on some rational end-point, and say for instance "people have sex in order to reproduce," are people you politely back away from at a party. For the rest of us, whether it is eating too many Haribo, gambling away our life savings, buying an SUV on a high-interest loan, or drunk-WhatsApping a crush, the tension between what we know we should do in our long-term interests and what we feel like doing right now is a common (and well studied) feature of human behaviour, and occurs especially in the context of activities we think will be pleasurable, cool, fun, and so forth. There's that drive towards things that promise they will make us feel somehow more awesome, more in control, more sated, that we can't always avoid listening to. Nor should we always listen to it, but it is in this sense — the capacity to make a larger sacrifice for a small reward — that I say we aren't always "sensible," and crucially it is according to this pattern that we must understand the widespread use of social media.

As I have said, the idea of individual responsibility is an important part of how politics, justice, morality, and even health are conceptualised, and is based on the idea that we can easily avoid doing illegal, self-detrimental, or injudicious things. Eating too much? Go on a diet! Not earning enough? Work harder! Going on Facebook for hours a day? Just use it less! Narratives abound about people "pulling themselves up by their own bootstraps" (physically impossible), or "snapping themselves out of it," but this is a barbarically unfair and myopic way to understand human behaviour. Not only are there structural and systemic issues in every society that often prevent easy answers, but individually we are not robots either — to be human is inescapably to be irrational.

Irrational use of social media has been the subject of considerable research. University students — being amongst social media's most voracious users — are frequently the test subjects of such experiments, so it should be no surprise that *procrastination* is one of several irrational uses of social media that are well studied. As nobody will need reminding, with procrastination there is a tension between a long-term "intended behaviour" and a short-term distraction (or many) that prevents or delays the intended behaviour from being carried out. While the aspect of procrastination that involves postponing or avoiding an intended behaviour is perhaps less relevant to the experience of using social media, it is essential that we learn what we can about the powerful irrational drive(s) involved in seeking distraction.

One particularly instructive study of Facebook procrastination amongst students, carried out in Germany by psychologist Adrian Meier and colleagues (2016), contains helpful reminders of some important aspects of the subject experience of social media use. Firstly, it finds that media stimulation from Facebook can be "hedonically pleasant," or in other words that people are tempted to use Facebook because it is pleasurable. This aspect of how we experience social media may sound obvious to some readers and contentious to others, but the fact that *pleasure* is part of the experience of social media for even a significant proportion of people should not be taken for granted. Given the web's historical characterisation as a practical, informational tool, it may be harder to admit that a website, or indeed an app, could or should actually be *pleasurable*. Over and over again, we are fed the idea that technology is invariably a faithful and unobtrusive tool that works for us. Tools are normally practical, and are usually sold to us as something useful and rational, but hedonic? When more conspicuously technological entities, such as robots or mechanical devices, are applied to basic acts of human life such as cooking, sex, health, or sociality, the most common response is suspicion, and rightly so as we resist the ongoing technologisation of our intimate lives. We recognise that pleasure occurs least often in automatic, predetermined, or technologised areas of our lives. Yet in social media we are happily welcoming massive technological edifices into our lives, our homes, our beds, our cars because they have found a way to be pleasurable without being too conspicuous. Technology being developed at the time of writing at Massachusetts Institute of Technology even uses sensors to detect the emotions of human beings when they are at home. "Researchers say that their so-called EQ-Radio devices can measure your heartbeat and breathing patterns to read whether you're excited, angry, sad or happy, with 87% accuracy," reports technology website *The Memo* (Knowles, 2016a). Chapters Four and Five will explore the implications of allowing technology to be so proximate to what matters to us, but whether or not we think of social media as pleasure for the sake of pleasure, it is clear that, for many, social media are a source of *enjoyment*.

Secondly, the procrastination study (Meier, Reinecke & Meltzer, 2016) argues that the primary draw of social media is not functional, but *dysfunctional*, and finds that Facebook is "often selected *impulsively* and *in an uncontrolled manner*" (emphases added). Again this will sound familiar to any regular social media users, but while it may be obvious, it is a significant characterisation of social media, because if the drive to seek a given pleasure is *automatic*, this suggests it is somehow beyond our control unless we apply conscious thought to it, requiring the additional effort of self-control, and that all-too-rare capacity of reflection on one's own behaviour. It is exactly this failure of self-control that permits procrastination and other compulsive social media use to occur:

> In many situations, users do not deliberately ponder over whether or not they should engage in media use (e.g. check their Facebook account). Instead, media exposure is initiated unconsciously through media habits […] More specifically, habits are characterized by automatic and impulse-driven initiation of behavior […] Thus the more habitually a medium is used, the more likely the medium is selected automatically and impulsively.

What this means is that even if your level of self-control is fairly strong, habitual use leads to further "automatic" (i.e. habitual) use, reinforcing the habit further still in a cyclical pattern, and eroding self-control that users might initially have had. Some research has even suggested that self-control is like a resource in that it can be depleted, leading to poorer decision-making (Wagner et al, 2013). To say that using Facebook is dysfunctional or born of a lack of self-control can be easily misunderstood to permit the deterministic arguments described above because it removes and externalises our agency, but just because your self-control may be weak in relation to things that you find pleasurable, that does not mean that the source of pleasure, be it Facebook or otherwise, has any direct power over you. As my students are sick of hearing me say, in order to be sure that they understand determinism, the reasons why you might eat a packet of Skittles are not within the packet itself; however much you might enjoy eating them, the Skittles themselves do not *make* you eat them.

The fact that social media use has the potential to be uncontrolled and automatic in this way has other consequences too. Some pleasurable activities, such as going out to dinner with friends, are selected and planned consciously, and can therefore be accommodated relatively easily by effective time management, but if conscious processes like self-control and time management are absent, automatic and uncontrolled use can potentially have a severe impact on the time we do have available, using up time that might be essential for other activities or responsibilities. One South Korean couple became so engrossed in an online game (games being another example of procrastinatory, hedonic media use) that they let their baby die of neglect. More tragically still, the game was itself a simulation of parenting (BBC, 2010). Thankfully, the same has not happened with social media, perhaps because they have less capacity to be so engaging, but the conflict between the time we have and the time we end up spending follows largely the same pattern.

The empty fridge

In Chapter One, I urged that rather than the posting and uploading of media — so-called "user generated content" — it is the *consumptive* use of social media to which we really need to pay attention. The necessity of this emphasis is partly because production and consumption are, as in economics, a single process that is ultimately driven by demand. Similarly with social media, these consumptive and productive activities can't entirely be separated, but this is precisely because they are mostly consumption-driven: We post because there is a chance others will see what we post; otherwise it is simply that proverbial tree, falling in the forest with no human being to "hear" it. But social media are not just any form of consumption: For reasons that will be outlined below, visiting and spending time on a social network needs to be understood as a form of consumption similar to that of other pleasure-oriented consumables such as junk food, alcohol, drugs, and pornography.

But what is it about the functionalities of social networks that might allow them to function in this way? Of all the innovations that have arisen as social media have developed, no more significant invention has appeared than the *timeline*; the roughly chronological, linear array of different "posts" or "tweets" containing a variety of different published materials. Facebook has one, Twitter has one, Instagram has two (sort of), LinkedIn added one some years after it launched, and YouTube's subscriptions and "Recommended" functionalities both largely reproduce this functionality. Even chat applications like WhatsApp can amount to a timeline when many people are all posting media, links, or spontaneous reactions to an informal group chat independently of any given user. Think of yourself scrolling down your Facebook feed. The most essential element of any timeline implementation is the user's sense of "what else is there? what's next?" You don't know exactly what your scrolling or clicking will reveal, but you know there will always be *something else*, and this provides you with an incentive not only to keep scrolling, but to keep coming back. Cast a sneaky eye over a stranger's shoulder on any given day on any given public transport system in any given metropolis, and you likely will see exactly this behaviour — endless scrolling, usually with the thumb. The exact form and underlying technological underpinnings may vary from platform to platform, and in some cases the functionality of a timeline is implemented more loosely, showing one post at a time rather than a list, and providing a user interface that allows the user to move from one item to the next in a more or less linear way. The endless stream of personal images on Tinder is broadly an application of the same idea, and the recommendations YouTube shows at the end of a video are also a good example of this architecture. The underlying pattern that involves continuous navigation of novel media is a hallmark of a social media timeline, and it is this architecture that reveals social media use as a form of consumption.

One very apt description of the dysfunctional and irrational relationship that we have with timeline-centric social media platforms, far better than Facebook's own bizarre and disingenuous claim to be "making the world more open and connected," has ironically appeared in "meme" form in the Facebook timeline itself. It reads:

> Facebook is like a fridge: You know there is nothing new inside but you check it out every ten minutes.

Admittedly, it was probably intended as a joke, but just as they say that in all the best comedy there is a degree of truth, the fridge simile turns out to be much more than a joke. The scenario above has even literally played itself out, or almost: One respondent in a psychology study that asked university students around the world to go without any social media for twenty-four hours reported that: "I literally didn't know what to do with myself [when I couldn't go on social media]. Going down to the kitchen to pointlessly look in the cupboards became regular routine" (Moeller, Powers & Roberts, 2012).

It may not have the figurative originality of Lady Macbeth's indelible spot of blood, Marx's base-superstructure, or John Donne's island-that-no-man-is, but the scenario of a slightly hungry person repeatedly checking a fridge (or cupboard) with unchanging and somehow unsatisfactory contents is surely a perfect allegory (although admittedly phrased as a simile) for many people's usage of social media. With the reader's permission, the idea deserves some unpacking.

Even in the case of literal hunger, forgetting for a second the comparison to social media, this pattern is a strange one. Fridges are where food is stored, so to visit them when hungry or even when seeking the pleasure of eating palatable food is understandable, but the repetitive action of checking the fridge while knowing that the situation inside it has not changed is not something a theoretically rational person would do. Articulated as a commentary on social media, the fridge comparison appears to recognise that in social media usage, as elsewhere in life, there is a *wanting* — an instinctive drive and desire that subordinates our capacity for logical thought. Just like how our desire for enjoyable food might drive our behaviour more than our logical certainty that we will still not find any adequate food in a fridge we have already checked repeatedly, our desire for… *something*… from social media also drives our behaviour more than logical thought.

The real question is, what is that something? For a hungry or stoned person, food is eventually the answer, but what is it that social media promise that could be comparable, and encourage the same type of pattern? What is the association in our heads that would lead us to feel we will find comparable satisfaction at a psychological, emotional, or purely hedonic level with that which food would provide? What are we hungry *for* when it comes to the social media timeline?

Critical theorist Walter Benjamin observed famously that whereas a concentrating person is absorbed by what they see, such as a work of art, the masses, who are merely distracted, absorb rather than are absorbed by what they see. Distraction and consumption, in other words, go hand in hand, and in the end distraction is something that can be consumable in itself. While the idea of distraction usually has a cognitive emphasis, which is to say that it is a change in your conscious attentions, the reason the distraction provided by the timeline is important is because of the emotional effects this change in attentions provides.

The social media timeline has been conceptualised widely as a news and information source, and has come to have an important role to play for the public sphere (the implications of which will be discussed further in the latter half of Chapter Five). However, far less has been said about how its content makes you *feel* — the subjective emotional experience of the timeline. This is strange, because the subjective emotional changes that result from the media you encounter, or what academics call *affect*, are inescapably its primary function. Affect can be thought of as the supercategory to which emotion belongs. Where emotion may properly be thought of as basic sensations such as fear, sadness, or jubilation, affect also includes a wider and more nuanced array of other subjective responses and states such as associations, moods, and reactions. Writing long before the inception of the social media timeline, journalism academic Todd Gitlin (2003) described the subjective experience of the "feeling of feelings" that occurs in media consumption generally. Besides being rational and informational, he wrote, media are "something we call *fun*, *comfort*, *convenience*, or *pleasure*. We have come to care tremendously about how we feel and how readily we can change our emotions." While some users might be logging on some of the time to find out what's happening, or to look for something specific, the social media timeline is relied upon far more often as a means for its users to manage their emotions. Some psychologists have developed the idea of people "managing" their emotions into a field called emotion regulation. Emotion regulation is defined by psychologist James Gross as "the processes by which individuals influence which emotions they have, when they have them, and how they experience and express these emotions. Emotion regulatory processes may be automatic or controlled, conscious or unconscious" (1998).

By allowing the user to encounter a stream of novel media stimuli from familiar sources, the timeline facilitates an easy way to *feel something other* than the emotions that the user would otherwise be experiencing at that moment in time. According to the research of psychologist Marvin Zuckerman (1980), this behaviour is called "sensation seeking." Human beings, psychologist J.H. Patton tells us, are "aggressive sensation seekers" (2014). This momentary distraction from the user's emotional reality provides an excellent means of emotion regulation. The appeal of the timeline for emotion regulation comes both from how it is structured and from the content itself as situated within that structure. The first place to begin understanding the timeline is to take a look at that content.

In so far as great books and films also make us feel something, we could simply consider the content of the timeline as another form of entertainment. But just as the timeline cannot be considered as purely an information source, to cast it simply as a source of entertainment akin to a novel or a movie would also be a superficial assessment. All entertainment to some degree gives its consumers something different to feel in the way that I have argued the timeline does, but other forms of entertainment mostly lack the features of the timeline, such as its uniquely interactive character and user-centrism. Each time you read a novel, for example, even if that novel is gripping at moments, even if that novel changes your life, the actual experience of engaging with it is not one that you seek under the table while at dinner, behind the wheel of a car, or furtively at your desk while you are at work. When we watch a movie it tends to be from beginning to end, and watched usually no more than once or twice. Even if we sense that a movie will be really good, its ability to entertain us is a temptation we can generally resist until the appropriate moment. Studies of our use of conventional entertainment can help us to understand our motivations for using social media, but we need to recognise that it would be a mistake to consider the timeline simply as a form of entertainment. If the timeline is a source of entertainment, it is radically different from other forms of entertainment in how it is mediated and constructed, and most of all in how it is consumed.

The different content items in a social media timeline all resonate emotionally to different quantitative degrees, as well as in different qualitative ways, but what is important is the fact that they resonate in a way that provides a form of emotional distraction that is pleasing to a given user and enables emotion regulation. The top hashtag on Instagram, for example, is *#love*, which has nearly a billion posts, almost double the number associated with next most popular tag. Some content is "feelgood" material that resonates with the viewer because it affirms positive or hopeful fantasies — for example, a destitute person unexpectedly receiving money or some other form of assistance by some random act of generosity; a person overcoming hardships "against all odds" to achieve some success or honour; a couple or a family being reunited against all probability; a person who has lied or cheated being exposed and receiving just comeuppance. Similar to standard entertainment, the same narratives tend to recur, often reinforcing ideology at the cultural level, but timeline media need not even have narrative at all in the way that other entertainment usually does, and it is partly their capacity to communicate something meaningful with virtually zero narrative that makes them so potent. For example, non-narrative media that produce an emotional response and might appear in a typical timeline could be: A sardonic cartoon about Brexit (despair and resignation), a video showing Dennis Bergkamp's five greatest Arsenal goals of all time (belonging and awe), a satirical clip about Donald Trump (disbelief and probably dread), the wedding pictures of a high-school friend (love, envy, or perhaps pity), a petition demanding that a UK supermarket chain sell only free-range eggs (indignation, aversion to cruelty), and a photo of a sunset, possibly enhanced with a filter (aesthetic enjoyment, possible envy).

Instead of the "feelgood" variety, content might also be alarming, outrageous, arousing, disturbing, surprising, humorous, or stimulate other emotions or combinations of emotions, which do not all necessarily need to be positive or happy. At the individual level, specific media will also be experienced differently by each user because they trigger associations and reactions that are different for each person. Neuroscientists have shown that cognition and affect can't ever be separated (Davidson, 2003). Your cognitive recognition of something and the associations that you have with it are what determine how you feel about it.

The precise feeling, however, doesn't need to be the same between individuals, it only needs to have the capacity to make the user feel something; to provide emotion regulation. Of course, the whole point of all media consumption is that it is emotionally resonant, but in the timeline this resonance is increased by the variation from one media item in the timeline to the next. The sensation is potentially very different with each image, movie, link, or update from a friend; this adds to the timeline experience. Posts from somebody you are in love with will play a very different role in the timeline from pictures of food you want to eat, yet what the two have in common is the very fact of a certain form of hedonic stimulation itself, even while the affective experience of each item will be different. If everything in your timeline is happy, or everything is sad, the emotional effect of this can push you too far in one direction, and nobody would check an overtly sad timeline.

A controversial study in 2014, carried out on Facebook without the explicit consent of its users, found that this effect went so far as to facilitate what it called "emotional contagion." Those who experienced more positive content were more likely to post more positive things themselves, and similarly those people exposed to negative content tended to post more negative things themselves. This is a reminder not only that the emotional responses we experience in relation to what we see in the timeline are enough that they have the capacity to alter our mood, but that generally the variation in how the different items in the timeline affect us is an important part of the experience, even if some of those posts have little effect on us at all (like this author and posts about rugby, *The X Factor*, or pulled pork recipes). Just keep scrolling!

As with the fridge meme above, there are moments where the content of the timeline "goes meta," and provides useful critique of the very same experience that it forms part of. One such example is a cartoon showing two figures: The top one shows a serious-looking figure with the caption, "Sharing status about economic, politics, government, and other relevant stuff to my country," and a single "like" thumbs-up icon. Below this, a feminised version of the same face, but made to look stupid with eyes pointing away from each other in different directions, is accompanied by the caption "Derpina went shopping." A corresponding "like" icon shows 4,458 likes and 980 comments. In the bottom section, a figure up-ends their desk in frustration at the discrepancy in response between the two status updates. Despite the casual sexism in this depiction, the "struggle" it shows "is real," so to speak: Content related to "serious" issues simply does not have the same appeal unless it can introduce some form of affective *sweetener* such as humour or outrage. Another example of this is the experiences of an acquaintance of mine whose job it was to distribute discount codes for different products every day on social media. "It's a lot harder to get 'likes' on toilet paper," she told me, than on hedonic offers like spa treatments and restaurant discounts.

Humour is consistently one of the most important emotional functions of the timeline that helps content achieve the resonance intended by its authors and those who share it. Amongst the dogs falling into swimming pools and "what my boss thinks I do" memes, humour is also one of the most effective vehicles for the communication of information and opinion about serious issues such as politics and climate change. Given the primacy of subjective affective experience, one might expect that conventional news and comment, usually connected with "factual" reporting, would no longer be part of what the timeline contains. Provided, however, that those who produce informational media are willing to "play the game" of affect-driven media, and incorporate affect such as humour into these media, informational content can still be popular. Indeed, humour provides a means of acceptable, if inadvertent, social commentary that avoids being preachy or sanctimonious, and often captures critiques that people would not necessarily think to make in sincerity since it is far easier to mock things than to argue with them. TV and radio shows like *The Daily Show* or BBC Radio 4's *The News Quiz* show that the use of comedy for factual, social commentary is far older than the timeline, but the affect-centrism of the timeline is an environs for such media to enjoy widespread popularity. *Al Jazeera*'s social media news arm AJ+ employs comedian Francesca Fiorentini to present their news videos not just because of her talent, but for exactly this reason: She's funny, and that gives their videos exactly what they need to achieve the affective impact that the timeline requires.

If informational media cannot be made to be funny, then other dominant affects can easily come to the rescue. Outrage and curiosity, for example, are also common vehicles in which information about the world often travels from one timeline to another. This in itself is not unique to social media. The sidebar of the *Daily Mail*'s website *Mail Online,* often referred to as the "sidebar of shame" and full of salacious, lecherous headlines is a classic example. But it likely accounts for why the website is the world's most popular for English-language news (Press Gazette, 2015). The social media timeline takes this same feature — a stream of novel, emotionally salient material — and makes it into the primary feature. While the ability to find things interesting is generally something that is undermined by the prevailing culture of consumerism, and the vapid "ten pictures of celebrities without makeup" content that it produces, outlets such as Vice News and AJ+ have managed to use both curiosity and outrage to great effect in distributing news media according to the affect-centric rules of the timeline. To the extent that some elements of the public sphere have been incorporated into the social media timeline, an understanding of affect-centrism is essential for the survival of factual media such as journalism. A number of examples have shown affect to matter far more than informational content. In 2012, the short documentary *Kony 2012* quickly began receiving millions of views as people became invested in the issues it raised, and the war crimes in Uganda it sought to prevent. But Joseph Kony, the Ugandan war criminal against whom the video was made, had left northern Uganda six years previously and life in the country had begun to return to normal. The film radically dramatised and simplified a complicated situation instead of prioritising the conditions on the ground in Uganda, arguably misrepresenting the issues to millions of people in the process. But that didn't matter, now millions of people around the world had learned that there was a bad guy called Kony who must be stopped. Another even simpler example is Hurricane Sandy, which hit the US Northeastern Seaboard in October 2012. Alongside the genuine eyewitness reports, images, and footage of the alarming realities of how New York life had been interrupted, collected by individuals with smartphones, were numerous fakes and spoofs. One anonymous Twitter account tweeted that the trading floor of the New York Stock Exchange was flooded, which was picked up by CNN, despite being completely false. Still images were taken from movies; others, such as sharks swimming at the bottom of an escalator or a diver in the flooded Times Square subway station, where the water is blue and the lights still switched on, were deliberate fakes, made with software such as Adobe Photoshop.

To illustrate to my students the ease with which these images can be created, I often create a similar image like the one opposite before their eyes using a picture of a platform on London's Victoria Line and a stock image of a diver, but the point is that the veracity of these images is irrelevant: The fantasy, the aesthetic, the entertainment and the social value of these images are far more important to users, and these are all part of a subjective, affective experience. The implications of this affective emphasis for the continuing challenge of spreading accurate news and information are serious, and are discussed further in the second half of Chapter Five. Suffice it to say for now, however, that whether we are enjoying debating the veracity of the image or getting angry at what it appears to portray, emotion is everything in timeline media. It's what keeps us scrolling, and what keeps us coming back "every ten minutes."

Another easily demonstrable case where our automatic affective reactions to media are heavily implicated in our consumption of them is in cat videos. Long mocked as a caricature of the inane sort of thing that people waste time looking at on the internet, and on social media particularly, cat videos are a phenomenon that have also been studied in a serious academic context. According to a study by psychologist Jessica Gail Myrick (2015), there were more than two million cat videos on YouTube as of 2014, with nearly twenty-six billion total views, and two film festivals devoted to internet cat videos, in Chicago and Los Angeles. Myrick found that cat videos not only were a popular procrastinatory form of media, but that they had the capacity to improve people's moods. "Levels of each self-reported negative emotional state measured in the study were lower and levels of each positive emotion were higher after viewing Internet cats," she tells us. "Beyond hedonic implications for viewing Internet cats, the data indicate that the excitatory potential of the [cat] content can also reduce depletion and energize viewers." Against the backdrop of this research, online sources such as Twitter accounts "Why my cat is sad," "Emergency kittens," and "Embassy cat" (which supposedly lives at the Ecuadorian Embassy with Julian Assange) reveal social media consumption, with or without cats, as being very likely an affect-driven means for managing one's emotions.

Anticipation and automatic reactions

There is a big difference between merely having an affective response to media that we encounter, which is unavoidable, and affect being the primary reason that we seek out the social media timeline. Besides the heavily subjective nature of how most of the media that appear in the timeline speaks to us, the encouragement on the part of the platforms to respond with non-verbal emotional gestures such as the like or the retweet, and there being very little else to explain the irrational, compulsive relationship that we appear to have with social media, we can also be sure that the consumption of media in the timeline is driven by affect because the reactions we experience to the media of the timeline are amongst some of the most potent feelings human beings can experience. Besides humour, belonging, curiosity and other common timeline media emotions, there is an even stronger affect: Anticipation.

Think of all the basic emotions that various religious people have told us to avoid over history — things like gluttony, lust, greed, envy, pride, wrath, and sloth. These are the things that connect us most with our most basic human selves, and that can release some of the strongest feelings, which is exactly why they have been forbidden by so many belief systems. They are also exactly the animalistic urges that Freud argued were often repressed in order that "civilisation" be able to function, hence the appeal of any media experience or platform that encourages them, albeit within restricted parameters. One of the more powerful affective sensations that the social media timeline provides the user with is *arousal*. As a major study of emotion and social media reported in 2016, "threads with emotional content lead to higher arousal than threads with neutral content" (Garcia et al, 2016). The word "arousal" is normally associated with the state one is in during sexual activity, but this is a far narrower meaning than the word is capable of. Arousal is actually a more general state of heightened sensitivity to an emotionally important activity and is defined in neurological terms as an increased activity in your sleep/wake system, unconscious bodily functions such as breathing and heart rate, and hormones, and as its similarity to the words "arise" and "arose" might indicate, its literal and original meaning means to be awake. Psychologists Byron Reeves and Clifford Nass describe arousal as "a volume level on things good and bad," and as "the *intensity* of experience, [which] ranges from feelings of being energized, excited, and alert, to feeling calm, drowsy, and peaceful" (1998). The feeling you get just as a waiter puts your meal down on the table in front of you and your saliva glands increase production, or the nerves right before you go on stage to perform, are forms of arousal just as much as the anticipation of sexual activity might be, even if less intense. The hormones released may be different in each case, and the social meaning of each is clearly different — indeed, the same stimulus may cause different arousal in different individuals, but neurologists have identified arousal as a singular state that all humans are capable of feeling, however subjective the effect of the stimulus. Rather than being an emotion in itself, arousal is usually considered to be the strength of an emotion.

One feature of the more visual elements of social networks that supports the idea that social media consumption may be partly arousal-driven is the high prevalence of *food images* on social media. The initial complaint about Twitter, just as it was catching on, that it was "just people saying what they had for breakfast" may have been short-sighted, but there were, and still are, an awful lot of breakfast images on there. Other social networks are similar — at the time of writing, there are nearly fifty million images tagged "#breakfast" and well over 180 million tagged with "#food" on Instagram. Like selfies, the desire to share what you are eating may well be driven more by performativity as far as the user's own experience of what s/he is doing, but the consumption and viewing of these media is the other side of the coin: We share certain content partly because we have also viewed such images, as well as the food they portray, and feel sure of the affective capacity of the former to excite us as if they were the food itself. This of course is ironic given that even a cursory scroll through the list of content tagged "#breakfast" on Instagram is an achingly banal experience.

Posting food images is not some obscure sideshow either: There are Facebook pages for almost every different type of food — even a page for those who want to "like" radishes, although at the time of writing it has only 356 "likes" out of over 1.79 billion monthly active Facebook users. When, for research purposes, I try to create a new account on social image-sharing platform Pinterest, having deleted my old account some years ago, "Food and Drink" and "Meat" are two of the most prominent "suggested" categories of image.

The depiction of things that give human beings pleasure and that appeal to our "forbidden" emotions is no accident, and is an important part of how we use the internet hedonically. The study of procrastination mentioned at the beginning of this chapter found, in addition to its other conclusions, that impulsive checking of social media "is particularly likely when individuals are confronted with *stimuli* that elicit strong *automatic reactions*" (Meier, Reinecke & Meltzer, 2016). What this means is that if some item we see on social media represents to us something that we have a strong reaction to because of a pre-existent relationship to it, such as food, it is more likely that we will check impulsively in the future for more such media.

That social media include representations that produce automatic or instinctive reactions in us — such as pictures of our friends in various scenarios, pictures of food, pictures of inexplicably adorable animals, or social drama of some kind — as one of their core features, should immediately tell us something about why we like them so much. The fact that these aspects of our environment are themselves psychologically active on us, and that we can't seem to stop looking at pictures and other media featuring them, is a further reminder that social media cannot be studied purely as a series of convenient practical tools, and that their appeal goes much deeper than that. The way social media distil psychological stimulation and emotional arousal into a consumable experience is what gives them their power.

Where there are valuable things to be learned about the relationship between human beings and the technology they have created or use frequently, we shouldn't be coy if some of the most important conclusions we could draw may come from internet media usage that is beyond the bounds of acceptable social, and, for some, moral and political conduct. If there is one context in which the hedonic consumption of digital media that have automatic psychological and neurological effects on their users occurs, it is in the use of internet pornography. Pornography use takes place on a massive scale. While for some it may just be a hastily closed browser tab out of sight, the pornography industry is worth ninety-seven billion dollars globally, dwarfing the main revenue for social media — advertising spending (which will be lucky to reach half that in 2017).

Alongside the "Food and Drink" and "Meat" icons on the Pinterest sign-up screen is the category "Curvy women" with its own icon. If sexual arousal and looking at images of food have nothing to do with one another, why are they on the same platform? What could be similar about the experience of looking at pictures of food and looking at pictures of "curvy" women? And why is Pinterest, which knows only my age and gender, so keen to show me them concurrently? Never mind the obvious objectification involved in reducing human beings to nameless "curvy women," why would I want to use the same media platform on the same computer, possibly even in the same session, to look at both food images and images of women with a particular type of figure? It says a lot about Pinterest's expectations of how I might use their platform, but is unlikely to be unique to that platform.

Food and sex are both central areas of human pleasure — one thing philosophers and scientists can agree about. Whether an image depicts food, cats, your best friends at a party, or something sexually resonant, it's possible that the same little voice somewhere in your brain says "oh hello — that looks like reward behaviour to me," and this connection is worth exploring further.

The same connection is probably made most explicitly by the term "food porn," which is a well-known genre of image. Especially in a digital context the term subtly reveals more than a simple metaphor. Even if inadvertently, it acknowledges that the hedonic viewing of media that features food you cannot eat might be in some ways analogous to viewing media featuring sex in which you cannot participate, with people you will never know.

There are over ninety-two million images on Instagram tagged "#foodporn," as well as several variants such as "#foodporno" and "#foodpornxxx." The most popular Facebook page by the name "Food porn" (there are several) has well over two million "likes." Interestingly, but perhaps unsurprisingly, it is operated by an agency called "Consumed Media." It features photos, videos, and recipes for food that is probably very tasty, but that is also clearly unhealthy and calorific. Some recent examples at the time of writing include balls of bread stuffed with cheese and coated with pesto, called "pesto cheese bombs," and several other recipes for food that is in some way or other stuffed with cheese. A comment from one of the page's subscribers on one of these posts reads, "You have done well today food porn." Another "Food porn" page with over two million likes shows pictures and recipes for cookies, burgers, and Nutella-filled cupcakes. Yet another one, again with over two million likes, features a short movie clip illustrating how to make a kind of burger sandwich labelled the "OMG roll."

Appending the suffix "-porn" to other forms of content also acknowledges that the hedonic consumption of visual materials is integrated into our most fundamental human drives. The comparison is not even limited to food. The suffix is also used for other types of visual content distributed via social media that are considered by some users to be particularly appealing. Some real-life examples are: A video showing people experiencing accidents or assaults immediately after having committed some deviant act themselves, labelled "justice porn"; real footage from fighting against the Taliban in Afghanistan shot with a GoPro camera, labelled "war porn"; a room stacked from floor to ceiling with firearms, labelled "gun porn," which is also the name of a Facebook page with over a hundred thousand likes; and a Facebook page consisting of typographically stylised phrases, sentences, and paragraphs bearing messages usually having to do with self-love and relationships, called "word porn," which has over eight million likes. The Twitter account @wordsporn has approximately 240 thousand followers, and somewhat amusingly, Twitter's heuristic algorithms seem to have taken the metaphorical comparison to real pornography at face value and provided a warning that "The following media may contain sensitive material." Only if you are allergic to *Sex and the City* quotes about loving yourself. As both a bass player and an occasional Instagram user, when I open the Instagram app I am invariably exposed to images of exotic and expensive bass guitars in all shapes and sizes, and featuring an alarming array of tropical hardwoods, usually tagged *#bassporn*, of course. Perhaps the most bizarre example I have regularly encountered on the web is that of "process porn," in which various industrial and manufacturing processes such as machine welding, moulding, laser cutting, extrusion, and computer numerically controlled machining are all rendered with perfect precision, albeit a predictable narrative. And there is no doubt that on some level it is at least intriguing to watch, for example, a sheet of iron cut by a laser into hundreds of tiny, perfectly formed pieces in 1.8 seconds, even as the voice of Karl Marx screams loudly in my head and the ghost of Frederick Winslow Taylor floats somewhere nearby. The technology world's obsession with 3D printing can be read as an extension of this same fetish.

I often ask students who study the psychology of digital media with me why they think "food porn" bears that name. The answers are usually quick, and always along the same lines. "Because it's a guilty pleasure?" offers one young woman. Having suspected from the "food porn" and similarly named pages that it might be worth investigating the psychology of pornography consumption in order to understand what allows other forms of digital media to be compulsive and hedonic, I could not help but chuckle when I first opened psychologist Dr Gary Wilson's illuminating book *Your Brain on Porn* (2015). Wilson is one of the world's leading researchers on pornography addiction and the validity of his work is supported not only by painstaking and difficult research, but by the fact that all the people who try to shut him down are invariably male freedom-of-speech activists who exude toxic masculinity like it's going out of style. There in black and white in Wilson's chapter on internet pornography, titled "Wanting Run Amok," was far more evidence of a relationship between pleasure, anticipation, digital media, and technology than I could ever have thought possible, and as we will see below, many of his words could almost have been lifted out of their pornographic context to describe Facebook use without any modification at all.

The most instructive sections of Wilson's chapter on online pornography focus on the neurotransmitter *dopamine*. Dopamine has many roles within the body, but most relevant to this discussion is that whereas chemicals known as opioids are responsible for the feeling of pleasure itself, dopamine is responsible for the motivation to *seek* pleasurable rewards. "At the top of our human reward list," Wilson says, "are food, sex, love, friendship and novelty. These are called 'natural reinforcers,' as contrasted with addictive chemicals." "Dopamine surges are the barometer by which you determine the [likely] value of any experience. They tell you what to approach or avoid, and where to put your attention," he continues. "The bigger the squirt [of dopamine] the more you want something. No dopamine and you just ignore it. High calorie chocolate cake and ice cream — a big blast. Celery — not so much." This sounds almost *too plausible*, and I wonder whether a JPEG image on one of the many "Food porn" Facebook pages showing chocolate cake and ice cream might have a similar effect, and whether that is the reason why the official Facebook pages for "Cake" and "Ice cream" have nearly seventeen million likes between them, while that for "Celery" only has a modest (but surprising) nine thousand. Wilson quotes: Dopamine is "your motivation and drive to pursue potential pleasure and long-term goals." Like food, sociality also appears to be connected to dopamine release, and researchers have found that the drive to achieve social status is also dopamine driven (Martinez et al, 2010). One of the most important lessons we can learn from the research that has been done on human reward-seeking, also seen in the patterns of how people use internet pornography, is the role of novelty, which is itself something the reward systems of the human brain crave alongside food, sex, love, and friendship. "Dopamine surges for novelty," Gary Wilson tells us. "A new vehicle, just released film, the latest gadget… we are all hooked on dopamine. As with everything new the thrill fades away as dopamine plummets." There is nothing in these words that is exclusive to pornography, and it is hard not to think immediately of the timeline.

Could it be that when we visit the emotional hamster wheel of the social media timeline, unsure of exactly what we will encounter but certain it will contain *new* content posted by our "friends," our brain is involved in a very similar but lesser version of what happens in the brain of an internet pornography user on a so-called "tube site"? Might social media use, with its "food porn," "process porn," and the like, be a more respectable version of the same behaviour; what Freud or Lacan would have called a *sublimated* version? This is at least a possibility that we need to consider.

There are of course many important critiques to be made, or which have been made, of pornography (West, 2016; Power, 2009;

MacKinnon & Dworkin, 1988). Ultimately, pornography is the site at which patriarchal capitalism extracts value from sexual objectification and often even degradation. It is usually consensual, and can even be well compensated, but all within a hegemonic, exploitative framework that prioritises the consumers and producers of such media far more than those portrayed in it, who are dehumanised and humiliated for a fee.

Whatever your feelings about pornographic material, however, this is not an argument about pornography; it is an argument about other media, informed by a consideration of how pornography is used. Rather than engaging directly with the content or social context of pornography beyond what we all know about it, we need only to acknowledge that it is psychologically and culturally salient material created for a form of hedonic personal consumption, via a private, digital, networked architecture.

In the context of this book, the important point is that online pornography needs also to be included in any serious discussion of psychology, technology, pleasure, and the internet, since it shows us that the relationship between hedonic pleasure and the internet is a much older one than social media and a far deeper one than we might be led to believe by the North American culture from which social networks have tended to originate, or its puritan origins. The argument here is not that social media are "like pornography," that the form of arousal experienced in conjunction with their use is the same, that they are used for the same purpose, or that the content of social media have the same cultural or subjective meaning as pornography. Neither is it my intent to naturalise or normalise the patterns of pornography use or social media use; quite the opposite — they must be seen precisely for their cultural specificity and psychosocial context, and the chapter that follows will situate them more firmly within that context. Like the eroticism of pornography, the resonance of all timeline media is both socially constructed and part of an individual subjective experience that reflects both the individual, and there is no necessity that any two users experience or use the timeline in the same manner, or respond in exactly the same way to the emotional stimuli in the timeline.

Rather, the point is that social media and online pornography both exploit similar aspects of the human subjective experience related to how people seek and anticipate novel pleasure from digital sources, especially in the absence of the genuine human relations that those sources appear to represent and portray. The fact that sex, friendship, novelty, and calorific food all stimulate the brain's reward system in comparable ways, and that the stimuli for these effects can all arrive via digital media, including social networks, means that our motivation for using any digital medium that appears to indulge these cravings is at the very least comparable, regardless of the specific content sought.

At least according to the naïve, primitive logic of the emotional brain, the promise of any basic and enjoyable form of pleasure, towards which psychologists would argue we are predisposed to turn our interests, is surely an enticing promise, even if an ultimately unfulfilled one. The relevant lessons that can be learned about social media from looking at research on pornography are therefore lessons about how our brain craves what it *anticipates* will be pleasurable, and how media technology that offers to provide it, without necessarily delivering it, can be used irrationally and excessively. It need not be the case that viewing pictures of highly palatable food is actually *as pleasurable as* eating actual food, just as few would argue that viewing sexual images serves as an adequate proxy for genuine sexual contact, that accruing Facebook "friends" is necessarily the same as having more friends, or that looking at images of cats is the same as having a real cat. As psychologist Barry Schwartz (2005) has observed, wanting something and actually enjoying the consumption of it are two dissociable affects. It is not the having so much as the *wanting* that is connected with dopamine, and the thrill, arousal, and anticipation that it produces. For that, images of what we want (or of what Instagram, Facebook, and Pinterest think we want) are enough.

Looking at images of food gives us a similar feeling, as if we were just about to eat that food, looking at pictures of our friends makes us feel as though we are about to see them, and looking at pictures of silly cats may even make us feel as though we will shortly be petting them (if only they would come a bit nearer). Anticipation itself, then, is a key driver of our consumption of the timeline; it is not the movie or the image, but the way it manipulates us into responding as though what it depicts is real and *about* to be ours that makes it pleasurable. As Marge Simpson's would-be lover Jacques once said in *The Simpsons* as he prepared to seduce her: "Better than the deed, better than the memory; the moment of anticipation."

Affective by design

Besides its content, the timeline has a number of structural and design features that are intended to make it as appealing as possible and to accentuate the social and affective value of its content. One such feature is in how we respond to the content contained in the timeline. While sharing and retweeting are multi-use gestures that allow content to be passed on for informational value, affective value, or any other reason, the "like" gesture is unambiguously an analogue of the user's subjective emotional response to the content they see, albeit within fairly narrow, if versatile, bounds. Originally developed by aggregator site FriendFeed, which was later bought out by Facebook, the Like button has been widely copied and interpreted on other platforms seeking to replicate the affective qualities of Facebook. Twitter even bizarrely converted their "favourite" button into a "like" button in order to make their implementation of this functionality more faithful to the similar buttons seen elsewhere. The fact that in 2016 Facebook expanded their version of this gesture into six responses — "Like," "Love," "Haha," "Wow," "Sad," and "Angry" — is an unambiguous confirmation of Facebook's own understanding of the timeline's primarily emotional orientation. Indeed, users had clamoured for years that Facebook implement a "dislike" button to enable negative reactions to the content they saw. The buttons could have been "Interesting," "Informative," "Relevant," and other more neutral descriptors, but they weren't and that is no accident. Buzzfeed, who publish content with titles such as "This One Question Quiz Will Tell You If You Actually Prefer Food Or Sex" that are designed especially for the timeline, also make a similar acknowledgement, allowing you to respond to their stories with six slightly different buttons: "Lol," "Win," "Cute," "Fail," "Omg," and "Wtf."

Another important feature of various versions of the timeline is the way that sociality is incorporated into the overall consumptive patterns that the timeline implements. After all, to emphasise the essential role of affect in timeline media and to take issue with the emphasis on sociality as a primary characterisation of social media is not necessarily to suggest that social media use or the consumption of media in the timeline do not occur in a highly social context. The sociality suggested by the name "social media" is not a complete misnomer, so much as a half-truth, and the media consumption and the social context in which it occurs are intertwined in a variety of different and important ways.

Because these media are shared publicly or semi-publicly, we consume them knowing that others with whom we share the same "friend" or the same interest in the form of a "like" or a "follow" can see them too, and we may get into conversations or participate jointly in reacting to a given item with individuals who are socially known to us to some degree. It is in these moments that the social nature of the timeline is apparent. As outlined in Chapter One, all media are social, and one of the main drivers for media consumption is the "water-cooler moment" in which we can discuss media with friends and co-consume. But it is also important to remember that such interactions are optional, and that the timeline can function very effectively as a private media-consumption platform with no water-cooler moment.

The fact that such sociality is optional is essential to the appeal of the platform. The architecture of the timeline incorporates the social context in which the consumption of the timeline's content, like most consumption, takes place. One of the interesting and subtle features of timeline-based social networks is structural ambiguity in how they combine public with private, social with personal. Users may even view media out of curiosity or outright enthusiasm that might put them at odds with social connections, and may need to suppress their reactions in order to avoid social consequences. Facebook, Twitter, Instagram, and other social networks report user activity to varying degrees. If my mum saw me "liking" fascist pages, for example, she might be a little bit perplexed, so I would need to be careful, but media consumption that might be considered deviant by our social connections is easy for all but the most novice users.

There is also the capacity for outright debate. If one of your friends posts something you disagree with strongly, you may initiate a debate with them and enjoy doing so because it provides the sort of affect you are looking for, while others might avoid getting into such a debate out of fear that they may damage the relationship with that individual or otherwise adversely affect their own social position.

If something can be both consumptive and social at the same time, it can fulfil two needs at once, increasing its appeal and relevance to everyday life. This kind of multiple purpose, especially given the entertainment, emotional regulation, arousal, and information value covered above that are also part of the timeline's consumption, hints at the extraordinarily broad role that social media have developed in modern life, which will be discussed further in Chapter Four.

Yet another important feature is the way that the timeline uses the scrolling mechanism of the devices used to access it. Scrolling is a functionality that has existed since the Seventies, but not until recently was it infinite, never mind so disconnected from the content being scrolled. The scrollbar used to show the length of the document being scrolled and the position to which you had scrolled; now it just jumps every time you get to the "bottom" once Facebook or Twitter has added more content for you to scroll, so that you aren't at the bottom anymore.

If items in our timeline don't elicit strong feelings, or don't elicit the right feelings, we are free to continue scrolling with seemingly little effort or investment. In this respect, the scrolling of the timeline is a behaviour similar to how users of cable TV in the 1990s used to "channel flick," popping quickly from channel to channel, assessing whether the TV program (or ad) on each was worth watching. The astonishing thing about watching somebody actually do this with cable TV was that nothing ever seemed interesting enough to keep watching; it was like the person was looking for something that was not really on offer. Social media timeline use is similar, and there is no guarantee that any of the items in the typical timeline will ever be sufficiently appealing, and thus no guarantee that anything you see in your timeline will provide you with the affective reward you so desperately crave. Ironically this is what provides the strongest reason to keep scrolling — that *thing* that you want to see, though you have no specific idea of what it is, could be just a bit further down if you keep looking for it, and Facebook, Twitter, and their friends surely know this. Worst of all, the less pleasing the items you do encounter, the more your ongoing usage needs to eventually produce a reward, since it is the reward "circuits" in your brain that are said to drive this behaviour.

What we actively seek from the timeline and the extent to which we are prepared to calibrate it by "liking" or "following" other pages are obviously different from person to person, but the inclination to keep scrolling is seamlessly accommodated by the infinite loading of more and more content, such that the scrolling need never end. Danish usability consultant Jakob Nielsen has long characterised use of the web as a "hunting" behaviour. His analysis is more based in the information-centric web of the Nineties, and so focuses on the idea of hunting for informational "solutions," but even if the solution hunted for in the timeline is affect, rather than information as in Nielsen's positivist, Nineties-flavoured analysis, the scrolling of the timeline is an almost perfect manifestation of what he described: Limitless discovery of new content and a fast means of assessing whether it is the desired "solution" or not. Unlike in Nielsen's analysis, this is a process that is anything but rational, and yet the interactivity of the experience, manifested in features such as liking, commenting, or scrolling further to discover new content, gives us a mistaken sense that we are in control. This mistaken belief in our rational, controlled relationship to the timeline — however subconscious — echoes the narratives that, as described in Chapter One, we have always been fed about the role of technology in our lives as something that *works for us*, and makes our "hunting" easier and more efficient, but this illusion is exactly what gives the timeline its power.

Other recent technological enhancements to the timeline have focused on making content from other websites fit more closely with the functionality and aesthetic of the overall timeline experience, and making the quick evaluation of the content encountered in that experience into an easier process. Facebook's implementation of auto-playing video, launched in 2013, meant that all video content, regardless of whether it was interesting or appealing, and even if it contained disturbing imagery, would start playing as soon as you scrolled to it. Not only did this expose users to potentially upsetting triggers, it sent mobile-phone bills rocketing because the broadband needed to buffer even the beginning of a video is so much greater than the proxy graphic that had represented videos before that. The feature can now be disabled, and video play starts off with the sound muted, but again the intention behind the implementation of this feature is not hard to see: Ease of consumption, to the point where it can even be inadvertent — you start watching a video you didn't even know you wanted to see because the first half-second of it looks promising. At the time of writing, Twitter has also announced that videos and animated GIFs uploaded directly to the platform will also auto-play. Instagram and Vine videos also start playing without the need for any user action, although with sound muted.

Twitter's "Card API" and Facebook's "Open Graph Protocol" are both technologies that make links to other websites appear in a far more visually appealing way, and further enhance the user experience of scrolling and evaluating timeline content. Facebook also implements an open standard called oEmbed that allows content from a wide array of other websites that also implement the standard to be interactive and immediately playable without any further action. The choice is always the same: Either consume now, or keep scrolling for something else.

The four essential qualities of the social media timeline

To summarise, taking both the content of the timeline and the architecture itself as a single subjective experience, the timeline has four qualities which together comprise a dramatic departure not only from the functioning of the "world wide web" in a historical sense, but from how culture and media themselves have been accessed, experienced, and consumed.

For a start, the timeline is composed largely of *familiar sources*, and gone is the anonymity of the early web. Everything from kittens to beheading videos is theoretically trusted and relevant to the user because it comes from a source that the user has selected. On Facebook and Snapchat, the familiar sources are your "friends" and/or the pages that you have "liked"; on Twitter and Instagram it is those people you have "followed"; on other channels such as WhatsApp groups that function similarly, it is the other members of the group. The familiarity of the sources you "follow" is what provides the timeline with its recurrent appeal; just like your friends themselves, the

familiarity of the timeline is a long-term one. A timeline composed
of items originating from complete strangers, after all, would surely
have far less appeal, and would represent a completely different use-
case. Our familiar lived reality is one we will do anything to extend
and reproduce over time, and the timeline uses the familiarity of our
friends, and to a lesser extent our certain chosen brands, to provide a
stream of media that we already know we trust. Even if many of these
sources are weak social ties such as old high-school friends, users
learn that as they scroll effortlessly through the seemingly infinite
timeline, the fact that they are acquainted with the person who has
authored, recommended, or shared that content means that they can
feel some sense of social connection as they consume or pass by that
content.

Secondly, the seeming *abundance* of the timeline is also a major
part of its appeal. Not only is abundance in itself an important
sensation that at a very deep level offers human beings reassurance,
it is constantly reaffirmed by capitalism as an essential and readily
consumable output of efficient production processes. The greater
the abundance, the more consumption is possible. The tendency
when we are faced with abundance is to gorge ourselves, and this is
exactly what we do within the timeline. As always when resources
are abundant, they are perceived to have lesser or no cost, but in
the case of media, that cost is time. The scrollable abundance of the
timeline means we are limited only by the time investment we are
prepared to make. That we may never actually discover content that
gives us the buzz we are searching for appears to the user only as a
limitation of the amount of time we are willing to spend looking for
it. Sociologist Judy Wajcman has argued that capitalism has a history
of using technology to transform our relationship to time. The true
cost of this activity (time) is de-emphasised by the seemingly limitless
abundance it appears to offer. This may not be the reason why the
"timeline" has been given this name, but like "food porn" or "social
media" it may be a naming that reveals more than intended about

its origins, and it is essential to recognise the power of the seeming abundance of available content.

Third is the *mixture* of different items that occurs in the timeline. Unlike earlier media distribution and consumption technologies, what the timeline architecture enables is a complete reconfiguration of media consumption; a custom-built media experience, constructed in real time by sophisticated, proprietary technology. To the extent that culture was already commodified before the internet, it usually had a time, a place, and/or a physical form in which this happened. Movies were in the cinema, for example, music in the club or concert hall, or on a record or CD, and news on TV at certain times or in a newspaper. The fact that music, images, video clips, links to text articles, and informal content from friends such as announcements and jokes are all available together on one web page or in one app, in a linear, scrollable form, is a revolutionary development for media consumption. The timeline is now an addictive hosepipe for the commodified culture and public sphere of its users, where people spend time at home, at work, or even in the middle of the night looking at whatever might be there, without the need to discriminate between these formerly separate areas of culture. The only important basis for discrimination is the emotion regulation that it provides. Commodification itself, or as the French more aptly call it, "uniformisation," is thus built directly into the architecture of the timeline. This development is part of a longer history of how the limitations in digital technology that stores and displays artefacts of human culture have forced a degree of sameness in the ways that information and culture are stored or displayed, meaning they have now been re-situated as merely "forms of content."

Lastly is the *novelty* it promises and crucially the unpredictability it uses in order that the experience of each visit to the website or app is different — and new — each time. Above I have highlighted the way that novelty is exciting and rewarding in itself, right down to a neurochemical level. This sensitivity is stimulated by the fact that there is no common narrative to the timeline. The fact that we do not know exactly what we'll find on the timeline means that right before each visit we cannot be sure whether there may be novelty or not, and feel the need to check, and this is the most important facet of social media that needs to be addressed. A clear separation can be made between forms of digital media that are used when somebody has a specific idea in mind of what content they are looking for, such as "how to convert to PDF" as a Google search or "Lion vs Tiger fight" on YouTube, and media that we visit simply to see what is new, or continue scrolling or interacting to see "what else" may be on offer. Whereas virtually all platforms that feature a timeline began initially by showing you what your friends had posted in reverse chronological order with the newest at the top, algorithms have now been introduced that select and reshuffle the items in your timeline and adjust their prominence so that even if you visit it twice in quick succession, you are not guaranteed to see the same content on both occasions. With enough sources, such as "friends" and liked pages, Facebook's algorithm — which is based on machine learning and reportedly takes more than a hundred thousand different factors into account — will likely not show you some items of content at all. Facebook has used an algorithm for years, while Twitter and Instagram both adopted algorithms in 2016, ditching the strict chronology of their previous architectures.

As psychologist Ciarán Mc Mahon (2015) has observed, there is a technique used for training animals known as *variable schedule reinforcement* (henceforth VSR) that follows exactly this pattern. When an animal is trained using VSR, a reward is provided on an unpredictable schedule, so that the animal does not know when it will be rewarded and when it won't. The animal hopes it will be rewarded in each instance, and thus repeatedly performs a given act (hopefully the one desired by its trainer) to check whether it will be rewarded. When the timeline contains such a variation of material that is rewarding in different ways and to different degrees, it is hard not to see the same variable schedule of reinforcement in play. You are incentivised to return to Facebook or Twitter again and again because you don't know what affect, if any, you will be rewarded with by the media you encounter on each visit. The timeline is not the only aspect of the social media platform that uses something very analogous to VSR either. The "notifications" feature of many social networks also may or may not show something upon each visit, and thus requires more regular checking. It doesn't matter whether it's a "like" from one of your friends, a quote, a comment, a share, a retweet, an update from a close friend, or the birthday of some random person you never talk to, there *might* be a new notification, and unless you check what it is for, you won't know, and unless you visit the social media platform, you won't know whether it is there at all. The repetitiveness entailed in the fridge comparison above captures exactly the idea of repeatedly returning to a place where you expect to find something rewarding, only to find the same underwhelming contents as before. What this suggests is that there can be persistent temptation without a rewarding or hedonic payoff, that the temptation, the wanting, can exist without theoretically *ever* being fulfilled. Even if there is some pleasure, one study has shown that guilt about having "given in" to temptation can effectively cancel it out: "the hedonic payoff from enactment was much larger for nontemptations [...] than the enactment effect for temptations which did not differ significantly from zero" (Hofmann, Kotabe & Luhmann, 2013). But even if we will not actually experience the timeline content in the rewarding way that is craved, this does not mean we can't *anticipate* finding something worthwhile all the same. A bit like searching for Prince's music on YouTube (which isn't there), looking for something that you are unlikely to find only heightens your sensitivity to and hunger for whatever it is you are looking for, increasing your desperation for an eventual payoff.

Whether or not you have succumbed to temptation or are simply killing time, the fridge may be full, or it may be empty, and you don't know if you don't keep checking. This uncertainty is of course where the metaphor breaks down. A real fridge cannot magically update its contents without some manual intervention. The social media fridge promises to be slightly different every time you return using sophisticated algorithms. Even if, in the fridge, the old slice of lemon, nearly-used jar of mayonnaise, and bottle of chilli sauce that you found there last time have now been replaced by an old carrot, a jar of mustard, and a tin of anchovies — equally unsatisfying items — there may at least be some all-important novelty to reward your visit. That means you have two powerful reasons to check: Not only do you never know when there might be an assortment of cupcakes in that proverbial fridge, or a jug of sweet lemonade, contents that will stimulate your arousal and provide you with a much craved blast of dopamine, but you don't know whether the contents will have changed at all, providing novelty. Thanks to the timeline's increasingly algorithmic nature, novelty is encountered more often than not, but this only strengthens the timeline's other possibilities: The most pleasurable items aren't there every time, and appear only just enough that you think it worth checking.

To argue that social media *train* us would be to regress to a deterministic argument, but the idea that those who designed Facebook, Twitter, and Instagram, to name a few, might have considered such techniques as their platforms were developed is far from inconceivable when it is recalled how valuable our usage of social media, and especially the timeline, is for social media enterprise. As will be explored in Chapter Four, social media are ultimately big business as an advertising channel, and the timeline is the main attraction. Hopefully it should also be clear that this crucial novelty element in social media does not contradict the familiarity mentioned above. The sources can be familiar, while the content itself is new, and it is still possible to seek novelty from a familiar source. Indeed, the idea of novel content from a familiar source is a powerful one. It is a long-held theory that capitalism must constantly represent itself as new, whilst simultaneously being trusted and familiar; here we see exactly this combination of features encoded as a hallmark of the social media timeline, but we are trained to seek novelty from familiar sources in almost every area of life, from "soup of the day" to Best Motion Picture to the newest Tesla model to software updates in the App Store.

Alongside an understanding of the timeline media's content as primarily emotional stimuli, the way in which these four elements combine as one simultaneous and unified experience explains an awful lot about why social media are so hard to resist. The timeline is designed to allow a number of important processes to occur simultaneously in a way that provides stimulation of an intensity that was previously impossible and convinces users that it will be intensely pleasurable, regardless of whether this is reliably true.

What pushes us towards social media?

More important than identifying these four features of the timeline is to ask why we appear to need so badly the social media edifice they comprise. The hedonic value of using social media outlined above might be enough to explain the use of it some of the time, perhaps idly "liking" the posts of friends for ten minutes here and there, but when millions of people spend hours on Facebook at the expense of their own wellbeing, we owe those people something better than the deterministic "technology X makes us do Y" explanation. Human motivation can commonly be understood in terms of a pull and a push working together; we are pulled towards something because of its own qualities, as described above, but in doing so we are often able to avoid or escape something else less pleasant. Now that we have examined the reasons why social media, and the timeline especially, might offer hedonic value as pull factors, it's important to ask: What needs does this consumptive pleasure fulfil within the functioning of human emotion, and why is spending an hour on Facebook better than spending the same hour away from social media — or rather, why do so many people think it will be?

Frequently we eat various foods, smoke, take drugs, and buy things we don't need because we believe it will feel good, and it usually does momentarily, but in these cases we are invariably using consumption to try and make ourselves feel better, and such hedonism is often about using distractions to escape, as Richard Wood has argued about video-game addiction:

> People will at times undertake all kinds of activities excessively if the activity has the capability to distract them from other issues in their lives. This is particularly true if the person concerned is having difficulty coping with other aspects of their everyday life. (Wood, 2007)

With social media, the notion of "escape" is perhaps a bit too spatial, given the history of "cyberspace" that is best left behind, but the scenario of fleeting engagement with stimuli that represent people, places, things, and events that are external to the immediately proximate emotional and physical reality of the user is not unlike escape. Whether we call it escape, distraction, hedonism, we are as motivated to do it as a means of avoidance as we are as a means to pursue pleasure for its own sake.

In so far as the things that make social media seem enticing can be understood by looking at other forms of hedonism and consumption, it's likely that there are also lessons to learn about what pushes us onto social media by examining what causes us to seek hedonism and consumption in other contexts. Food is also a good example of how stress produces irrational behaviour. Just as food intake has been relevant to social media use because of how both food and social media interact with the brain's reward systems in a hedonic way, social media also have something in common with food in terms of how their use is driven by stress and other negative emotions.

When people are unhappy (scientists refer to this as an experience of "dysphoria"), they also tend to lack motivation even to effectuate the things that are in their control, never mind to challenge the things that are not. When somebody is coping with stress, anxiety, or grief, for instance, they may feel less able to imagine the positive outcomes of any efforts that they might make, decreasing the motivation to try. Not only does this make it harder to ameliorate such circumstances, it can push us towards behaviours that make things worse. When faced with this type of low motivation that originates in negative affect, we find it harder to do "what's right" and easier to do things that make us feel good, albeit with a price to pay. Even rats show this effect (Coccurello, D'Amato & Moles, 2009).

When it comes to food and stress, the scientific consensus is generally that under-eating is the most significant marker of stress (Stone & Brownell, 1994), but when the available food is highly palatable or calorific, over-eating becomes a stress-induced behaviour (Adam & Epel, 2007; Torres & Nowson, 2007). Some scientists now suspect that visceral obesity (excessive fat around the abdomen) is an adaptation to stress (Drapeau et al, 2003). Interesting research on the idea of "comfort food" has revealed that some of the pleasure that arises from eating hedonic foods may go beyond the palatability of the food and actually have a therapeutic effect on negative affect and loneliness. It turns out that comfort food may have a genuine psychiatric basis and be comforting because it reduces loneliness and makes us feel closer to loved ones, with whom we associate that food:

> A move away from home, a fight with a close friend, a breakup with a romantic partner, and many other circumstances can leave one feeling alone and isolated. When these things occur, the "embrace" of a familiar food can be particularly alluring. (Troisi & Gabriel, 2011)

What all this research suggests is that when we experience negative affect, the balance between our desire for hedonic (i.e.

pleasurable) momentary rewards and our motivation to avoid things that are bad for us in excess is tipped in favour of the former. The relationship between stress, hedonism, and possible self-detriment is a recognisable pattern in many areas of life beyond what we eat. Stress can lead us to seek the momentary pleasure of sensation and consumption, even if these effects do not last. People more predisposed to stress by various individual factors are more likely to become and remain smokers of tobacco, for example (Kassel, 2000). Unhappiness and emptiness cause people to seek salve, comfort, and fulfilment. Indeed the availability of various forms of pleasure has always existed to mitigate the darker sides of living in an organised society. This aspect of our behaviour extends to how we use social media.

Psychologists trying to diagnose the broader and older phenomenon of internet addiction, distinct from social media use but comparable, have suggested a theory of what they call "compensatory internet use." Psychologist Daniel Kardefelt-Winther tells us that "The basic tenet of the theory of compensatory internet use is that the locus of the problem is a reaction by the individual to his negative life situation, facilitated by an internet application." The idea of the theory is that what people may be compensating for can be different from person to person: One individual may feel that they have no friends, and go online looking to make social acquaintances, while another may be bored and go online seeking entertainment. When the internet more generally, and perhaps social media more specifically, are used to make up for things that are otherwise absent from everyday life, at least in sufficient amounts, an important question arises: If looking for social connections is a compensation for not having enough friends, and entertainment is sought as a solution to boredom, what are hedonism, novelty, and reward sought for, and where do they fit within a compensatory model? If we are to understand social media as also being partly compensatory, then it would be inevitable that dysfunctional or compulsive social media use would be more likely in a context where the lives of its users are not particularly happy or fulfilling. In fact, this is exactly what the research is beginning to show: One recent study found that individuals who were happier showed significantly better self-control in relation to social media use (Wenzel, Kubiak & Conner, 2016). The research in this area is conflicting, and motivations that derive from people's private affect are very difficult to measure precisely because they are so subjective.

The real question, then, is what are we using social media to escape from and to compensate for? What connects a university student procrastinating working on an essay by looking at Facebook, an isolated young mother at home with a newborn who can't help spending hours on Instagram, and a depressed, unemployed drama graduate? The answer is emotional distress, whether acute or chronic, but we can and need to go further. It's too simple to say that everyone who is unhappy is unhappy for different reasons. Obviously the boredom of a university student, the social isolation of a single parent at home with a baby and the futile emptiness of a disillusioned performing arts graduate are both circumstantial and different from one another, but these are foreground affects that point to a deeper, more systemic malaise that is shared by all three. At a time when abuse of prescription opiates is at an epidemic level in the United States, and depression is amongst the most treated mental-health concerns in several developed countries, it is not hard to see that there may well be a link between widespread, chronic, negative emotional disposition and equally widespread social media use. An understanding of sensory pleasure and broader societal patterns of unhappiness from which that pleasure becomes an escape, is an essential pattern for us to understand.

— THREE —

#FirstWorldProblems

Emotional distress and capitalist realism

Tell me are we unhappy?
Are we unhappy?
Are we unhappy?
We could be happy too.

Jam City aka Jack Latham, *Dream a Garden*

You don't hate Mondays, you hate capitalism.

Facebook meme

Society everywhere is in conspiracy against the manhood of every one of its members.

Ralph Waldo Emerson

If the hedonic use of social media is driven by the emotional compensatory patterns I have described in the previous chapter, that would suppose that many of the 1.18 billion people who, at the time of writing, check Facebook every day, for instance, are in enough emotional distress of some form that they need the emotional regulation that I have argued social media provide. But is this likely, and how can we be sure? Even if only half of social media users consume social media content according to this pattern, there are still important questions to ask about what these hundreds of millions of people are escaping from. We all have our bad days, but what could be making so many people seek the compensatory emotional regulation I have described, and to such a degree? There are more potential answers to these questions than can ever be sensibly analysed together in one chapter of one book, and anyway, doesn't everybody who experiences emotional distress, be it loneliness, depression, anxiety, or similar, have their own personal reasons why that may be the case? Yes and no. While this may be true on the surface, the distribution of emotional distress also follows societal and cultural patterns that are helpful when drawing a bigger picture of how people compensate for these feelings, whether with retail therapy, opiates, or social media. This chapter is about those patterns.

On a 2013 episode of US late-night TV show *Conan*, US comedian Louis CK said:

> You know, underneath everything, in your life, there's that thing, that empty... forever empty... [to Conan O'Brien] you know what I'm talking about? [...] There's that knowledge that it's all for nothing and you're alone. You know — it's down there. [...] And sometimes, when things clear away, [...] you start going "oh no, here it comes, that I'm alone..." Like, it starts to visit on you. You know, just this sadness. Life is tremendously sad just by being in it. (September 20th 2013)

Perhaps we so often need to hear the most poignant and important things from comedians precisely because this role gives them a greater license to point out gently the most serious truths of all, but for most people it will be very difficult to read these words and not have any idea what Louis CK is talking about. It just isn't easy being conscious and mortal. Beyond this nearly universal feeling, known as abjection, life in most early twenty-first-century societies can consist of quite a few other negative emotional experiences for which we might be compensating.

Before speaking about the emotional reality of society or culture, especially in relation to technological features of life such as social media, some clarification is needed: Which society are we talking about? While internet access is obviously not as easy in some regions of the world as others, social media are a global phenomenon, used by people from virtually every country, and from many different backgrounds. As a major global study published by anthropologist Daniel Miller and colleagues at University College London in 2016 has shown, it is a mistake to assume that the use of social media in all these societies is the same or has identical motivations (Miller et al, 2016). This is also true of emotional distress, and one can't just talk about "people," "society," or "culture" in general, especially when the number of potential people involved runs into the billions. A firm analysis of the connection between negative emotions and any type of media use is far more likely if people are grouped together by what they have in common in fairly large groups. If there are certain societies having significant aspects of their cultural and political life in common that also show similarities in how social media are used, then that is a far more useful and instructive outcome.

The arguments advanced in this book will therefore aim to situate compensatory social media use in relation to specific forms of emotional distress that are common in the most developed, industrialised countries, such as those in Western Europe and North America — what economist J.K. Galbraith (1999) called the "affluent society". The reasons for this focus will become clear, but nonetheless it should be stated explicitly before going further that this emphasis is not born of disinterest in or disregard for other regions; nor are other regions imagined to use social media significantly less. In fact, according to research agency We Are Social, the country with the top Facebook usage penetration rate in 2015 (percentage of population) was the Philippines, followed by Mexico and Turkey. Rather, this focus is because, as we will see, there is a relationship between exactly that predicament of being what we could call an "overdeveloped" society and the particular emotional states that drive the variety of compensatory media use I have suggested.

The idea that life in wealthy, industrialised societies might impact our mental and emotional health negatively is one that many people find counter-intuitive. One of the many myths about contemporary life on planet Earth that we are repeatedly asked to accept is that since life in the developing world is often a grim struggle for daily survival, life in the developed world must be pleasant, easy, and happy. The *#FirstWorldProblems* hashtag from which this chapter takes its name, an open conversation that satirises the overprivileged gripes of first-world inhabitants, is primarily a communication of exactly this idea: There are no problems in the so-called "first world" except *#FirstWorldProblems* such as: "There's too much food in the fridge and no space for my almond milk," "Sorry I'm late. I missed my subway stop because I was busy working on my dog's Instagram page," or "Pokémon Go deleted my account :(" (all real examples).

Life in much of the developing world can indeed be grim; according to the World Health Organisation, half the developing world still does not have access to basic sanitation, and 1.1 billion people don't even have access to clean drinking water. A report from the World Bank estimates there are still over a billion people living on 1.25 dollars per day or less, and according to a report by Oxfam in January 2016, the richest sixty-two people on Earth own as much as the poorest half of the world's population. The injustice of this situation is so obvious it barely needs pointing out, but acknowledging this urgent and horrific state of affairs does not mean that the so-called "first world" can't also have problems. To put it another way, critiquing aspects of life that are related to exactly the forms of "development" that the developing world is said to lack does not mean that there aren't issues in the developed world that are not only serious, but which — as we'll see below — are caused by the very conditions that constitute being part of the "first world."

Admittedly, people do whinge regularly about relatively trivial aspects of first-world life without remembering that they are altogether nice problems to have, and this failure to recognise one's own privilege may indeed merit merciless satire, but we should not let these daft utterances or the running joke we have at their expense convince us that living outside of the developing world limits your right to critique the conditions in which you live, or that these are the only problems that occur there. There are *#FirstWorldProblems* and then there are real first-world problems, and yet it may be that the true first-world problems simply don't have a name, because we don't expect to find them or are encouraged by first-world culture not to look for them.

Many people in the developed world survive psychologically by using aspects of the material conditions in which they exist to convince themselves they are happy and contented with their lives. You've got an iPhone or a relatively new car — how bad can life be? In an age where depression is amongst the most-treated health conditions (UK) and opiate addiction is widespread (USA), we need to ask whether we're as happy as we want to believe we are. To understand how and why aspects of life in the developed world might be implicated in emotional distress, and how in turn these feelings may drive social media use, we need a good picture of what the emotional reality of so-called modern life really is.

These are often unpopular questions to ask, but there is genuine emancipatory potential in asking honestly whether there might be broader features of our day-to-day lives in the developed world that cause the long-term emotional health of our societies and cultures to suffer. Instead of the types of problem satirised by the *#FirstWorldProblems* hashtag, what this chapter will therefore outline are some of the genuine issues of life in the over-developed world and how they might create forms of emotional distress that directly drive people towards pathological rooms of media consumption such as compulsive social media use.

Real first-world problems

When we think of so-called "first-world" life, what do we think of? Besides increased consumerism and a greater level of material comfort on the whole, answers tend to relate to a strong social contract, such as democracy, welfare (to varying degrees), literacy, technology, and a free press. As Swedish development researcher and professor Hans Rosling has reminded us (2007), the ideas we have about what development, or lack thereof, actually means aren't always accurate. Philosophers Michael Hardt and Antonio Negri (2001) also take issue with the idea of "development," arguing that it suggests a destination towards which "developing" countries are moving (or should move), while "developed" countries have arrived. As we will see below, their theory is useful, and the differences between the "developed" and "developing" regions of the world are far more complex and far less teleological.

Be that as it may, our systems of government and the political health of our societies are generally implicated in our everyday mental wellbeing. There is a reason why self-determination, the freedoms of speech, conscience, thought and religion, and the rights to privacy and due process of law are all considered to be human rights and not luxuries (although too often they become luxuries). Without the security that these bring, we suffer existential anxiety and fear, and studies show that factors such as low crime rates and universal access to healthcare are positively correlated with good mental wellbeing.

To equate only basic social and political position with the overall psychological wellbeing of a society, however, would be to say that societies where people are relatively assured of these rights and freedoms are likely to be psychologically healthier, but it is not as simple as that. Sigmund Freud wrote famously in *Civilisation and its Discontents* that the repression of more animalistic urges (such as murder, rape, incest) that is required in the building of a safe and secure society actually *produces* psychological tension in itself. Obviously we find these actions morally deplorable, but as has been written about at length in the field of psychoanalysis and critical theory, the realms of what we want to do — usually oriented around reward behaviours such as sex, food or drugs — and what we are actually allowed to do by the social structures and conventions around us, exist side by side. As the threshold between them shifts incrementally in one direction or the other over time, the tension between them is exacerbated. Even in the case of lesser behaviours that may be pleasurable to some whilst deplorable to most others, almost every society has created rules about what can or cannot be enjoyed or disdained. Social acceptance and respectability arguably remain dependent on achieving the correct balance, even in an age of far greater cultural relativism: Enjoy or disdain the wrong things, and you will quickly be jailed, ostracised, or have your Instagram account suspended.

"The stock market is founded on greed and fear," British investor Mark Goodson said in an Open University documentary about the moment the so-called dot-com bubble "burst," but the reverse is also true, and economics play a major factor in our emotional wellbeing. In economic downturns, for example, people lose their jobs and begin to commit suicide in significantly greater numbers. A study of fifty-four countries, published in the *British Medical Journal* (BMJ), showed that in the economic recession of 2008–09, suicide rates increased significantly and were correlated with the levels of unemployment that resulted from the recession (Chang et al, 2013). Interestingly, the study found that this was more likely amongst men, young people, and in places where there had previously been low levels of unemployment. More worryingly still, a linked analysis of the same study, also published in the BMJ, found that "this increased risk [of suicide] may have been carried forward in later years to the next age band — that is, that there was a 'cohort effect'" (Hawton & Haw, 2013). In other words, the increased risk of suicide that correlates with recession does not simply go away when the economy returns to growth; it may last longer than the actual recession. As the study says, this is particularly concerning given the already increased impact on young people.

Government policy and economic conditions are not necessarily separable sources of causation when it comes to emotional wellbeing either. It will not come as a surprise to many people that governments and markets do not occur in parallel universes. Government measures taken in response to economic recessions can have significant knock-on effects on how the recession affects a given population, including on the number of people who take their own lives. The second BMJ study quoted above remarks that:

> It seems that where governments choose austerity measures to tackle national financial debt the [suicide] impact [of recessions] is worse. In contrast, active programmes to keep as many people in work or other meaningful activity and to support community healthcare and benefits can reduce or even fully counter these effects. (Hawton & Haw, 2013)

Not only do some governments not take such active steps to mitigate the psychological toll of recessions, they sometimes implement policies that make it much worse. In Britain after the last recession, the UK government's Department for Work and Pensions introduced sanctions on some of the country's poorest people in an attempt to coerce them off benefits and into the workplace, leading to suicides in many of these cases too. Giving people "meaningful activity" to do does not mean forcing people to work when they may not be able to, or suitable jobs may not be available.

Economics, it should now be clear to see, are not only a concern for people in suits. It is without doubt then that global recessions, government policy in response to them, and their correlation with suicide or poor mental health are clearly matters for concern when it comes to the emotions of the public, but this pattern may in fact be the proverbial "tip of the iceberg" because it is more noticeable than other forms of emotional distress. In all sorts of ways, economics affects the background against which everyday life occurs for ordinary people.

The extent to which economics affects everyday life goes well beyond economic downturns and fiscal policy, and turns out to have a much more far-reaching qualitative impact on our way of life.

To start with economics or culture and end up with widespread emotional distress may seem like a big jump, but their connection is by no means tenuous. These aspects of our lived experience have a far stronger impact on the emotions of their subjects than we realise. Such connections are not in themselves a new argument, and the role of culture or the economy in producing emotional distress has been outlined elsewhere, such as in the work of Mark Fisher (2009), Oliver James (2008), or Erich Fromm (1955), whom James quotes at length. While these arguments may not be original in themselves, they still need to be communicated and built upon until they are well understood and commonplace beyond specialist circles. Without wishing to reinvent the wheel, the next part of this chapter will be a brief account of the various ways that life in capitalist culture can be emotionally distressing, and how these combine to create an emotional "void."

The late capitalist workplace

The relationship between employer and employee is changing in ways that are highly relevant to emotional wellbeing, and the workplace therefore serves as one of the most useful and instructive means to understand the processes that large numbers of people have in common about the way they live.

It will barely need pointing out that in any contract of employment, any given worker is almost always more expendable than the employer. This gives rise to a power imbalance, because where workers can't afford to lose their livelihoods, the loss of a given individual, unless a highly sought-after executive, makes little long-term difference to the employer. This is a dynamic that has intensified over time, and the terms on which we are employed have come to favour our employers ever more.

At one end of the scale, an increasingly common employment basis known in the UK as "zero-hours contracts," but also prevalent in the United States and other countries, ties workers into agreements whereby they are not guaranteed any work at all week-to-week. Any hours they are assigned must be worked, or the worker will likely be dismissed or sanctioned, yet these contracts sometimes contain "exclusivity clauses" that forbid the worker from taking on any other employment, even when no hours are offered by the contracting employer. This sort of arrangement is obviously cheaper and more flexible for employers, but for workers it means lower pay and most crucially of all, more pressure and less certainty.

While governments are often happy to boast about any fall in unemployment, the statistic they frequently fail to mention is the one that relates to *underemployment*. If you are employed on a zero-hours contract, you count as employed, even if you didn't work any hours this week or last week, and may not do so next week either. While unemployment has indeed fallen on paper, the number of people precariously underemployed, whether on zero-hours contracts, in part-time work, or freelancing, has grown, and in a culture that tends to blame and stigmatise poor people for their own misfortune this change has quietly affected record numbers of people, and especially those aged eighteen to twenty-four.

To some extent, our culture is happy to accept the fiscal poverty of the young and the unskilled, seeing it as an "incentive" to work hard and consequently avoid poverty. Hard work is not an automatic ticket out of poverty, however. In December 2015, an investigation by the *Guardian* found that workers at UK sports-equipment retailer Sports Direct, despite working long hours, were often being paid at an effective rate below the minimum wage. The company, whose shares feature in a number of UK-based pension funds, was so worried about theft that employees were subjected to rigorous and often intrusive security checks. Since there were long queues and delays during these checks, and they took place outside clocked hours, they effectively extended the amount of time at work and correspondingly lowered the effective hourly rate, saving millions of pounds on the company's wage payments over the year. Workers were also reportedly so terrified to take time off work that they would send their children to school when ill, or not be at home when their children returned from school.

Another *Guardian* investigation in 2013 detailed shocking conditions at a "fulfilment" centre for online retailer Amazon in Swansea in the UK. As I write this I consider the irony that you the reader are reading criticism of Amazon in a book you possibly ordered from that same company. If you bought this book from Amazon, thank you all the same for buying it, and now let us spare a thought for the human being who so lovingly retrieved it from a box, placed it in a cardboard wrapper, and sent it on its way to your letterbox or doorstep. Amazon warehouse employees, who earn minimum wage, often work shifts up to fifty hours per week, and are reportedly sacked if they take three sick breaks in a three-month period — something the company denies. Employees are warned when they start that they may walk up to fifteen miles per shift, the warehouse being a quarter-mile long. Amazon also operates what Carole Cadwalladr, the journalist who carried out the investigation, calls an "apartheid" between different classes of worker. Permanent workers, who have a blue lanyard, receive a higher hourly rate of pay and are given share options in the company after two years. Temporary workers, who have a green lanyard, are kept in a precarious state. One employee told Cadwalladr:

> I worked there from September 2011 to February 2012 and on Christmas Eve an agency rep with a clipboard stood by the exit and said: "You're back after Christmas. And you're back. And you're not. You're not." It was just brutal. It reminded me of stories about the great depression, where men would stand at the factory gate in the hope of being selected for a few days' labour.

Both the Amazon and Sports Direct exposés are worth reading fully, but they are by no means isolated cases of employers imposing the harshest possible terms of employment on their workers in ways that reinforce their position as highly precarious and disempowered, and intensify the fear and emotional distress that accompany this situation. UK food delivery venture Deliveroo, who treat all workers as self-employed contractors and pay them well below the living wage, even colluded with the UK Home Office in July 2016 to check the immigration papers of all delivery staff at the Islington training centre, leading to the removal and arrest of three of their own trainees. The *Guardian* reported that in the same month, UK hamburger chain Byron "trapped kitchen staff in an immigration sting by calling for a meeting about cooking burgers." (O'Carroll & Jones, 2016)

Cases like these illustrate the capacity for work to be at once precarious, uncertain, highly pressurised, and above all, emotionally distressing. This type of shift has not only happened in so-called "unskilled" proletarian labour either; university lecturers ("professors" in the US), might once have been thought of in their ivory towers, but they have been increasingly subjected to a set of processes over the same time period that are analogous to what happened at Sports Direct. In fact, after an investigation by the *Guardian* into the use of casualised labour in UK universities, some of the UK's most prestigious universities were accused by union leaders of "importing the Sports Direct model" (Chakrabortty and Weale, 2016) In 2015, a video called "Professors in Poverty" highlighted the increasingly commonplace situation of individuals in the United States who hold advanced postgraduate degrees and teach at universities being paid so little that they needed to be on welfare in order to make ends meet.

At the time of writing, universities across the UK have been locked in a dispute with their employees for several years over pay stagnation and increasing casualisation. Literary scholar Marina Warner, writing in the *London Review of Books* in 2015 about the transformation of university life, quoted a letter she had received from a professor who had resigned from a Russell Group university:

> The incessant emphasis was on cash: write grant applications rather than books and articles in order to fund one's research … accept anyone for study who could pay, unethical as that was especially at postgraduate level, where foreign applicants with very poor English were being invited to spend large sums on degrees … Huge administrative duties were often announced with deadlines for completion only a few days later. We had to spend hours filling in time-and-motion forms to prove we weren't bunking off when we were supposed to be doing our research and writing during the summer "vacation" … It was like working for a cross between IBM, with vertiginous hierarchies of command, and McDonald's."

Again, we see less certainty and security, and more pressure, both in the actual work and in life more generally as a result of the decreased certainty. Across the board, in countless industries, the expectations placed on workers have gone up, while pay has often either stagnated, decreasing in real terms, or actually been cut. What seems like good business sense for the employer — flexibility and reduced costs — creates emotional distress for workers, and there is often no sense that workers are anything other than resources, there to be mined and exploited. This doesn't just concern conventional matters such as pay either. Particularly in the case of female employees, sexual identity is a common aspect of how workers are degraded. A 2014 survey of five hundred managers, reported in the *Guardian* in 2014, found that 40% avoided hiring women of childbearing age so that they could avoid the statuary requirements around maternity leave, despite this hiring practice also being illegal (and grossly unethical). In October 2016 it was reported in the *Evening Standard* that a London recruitment firm specialising in roles such as flight attendants and receptionists was even specifying requirements for female applicants such as attractiveness and bra size. One advertisement stated that applicants should have "a classic look" and "brown long hair with b-c cup."

Technology, alienation and neoliberalism

The fact that post-internet technology-based businesses like Amazon are often best placed to implement such changes to the terms of employment should be no surprise. Amazon's experimentation with drone-based unmanned delivery was as predictable as Uber's investment in the use of self-driving cars. As Harry Braverman famously wrote in *Labor and Monopoly Capital* (1974), the role of technology itself in the way work has changed is a significant one, and developments in technology are often driven by capitalist demand for new or different forms of labour, dehumanising and degrading the worker more and more. Sociologist Arlie Russell Hochschild's account of hiring practices in Silicon Valley, quoted by Zygmunt Bauman (2007), illustrates the early history of how technology businesses made more demands on their employees:

Since 1997, a new term – "zero drag" – has begun quietly circulating in Silicon Valley, the heartland of the computer revolution in America. [...] More recently, it has come to mean "unattached" or "unobligated". A dot.com employer might comment approvingly of an employee, "He's zero drag", meaning that he's available to take on extra assignments, respond to emergency calls, or relocate any time. According to Po Bronson, a researcher of Silicon Valley culture, "Zero drag is optimal. For a while, new applicants would jokingly be asked about their 'drag coefficient."

Businesses like Uber or Deliveroo exemplify the ways in which the smartphone, the database, and technologies such as GPS can be combined in the service of more customers, more profits, but never for happier or healthier employees. Karl Marx argued repeatedly that the more the capitalist mode of production advanced, the more impoverished workers would become. In the incorporation of new technology into the workings of business, we see exactly this tendency played out. Work in a capitalist economy is always a process of extraction and exploitation; even so-called "workplace wellness programs" that help workers stay fit emphasise the physical health of workers in the belief that this will make them more productive, but few questions are asked about whether the long hours, more accurate metrics and improved organisation that such technologies enable (and that such businesses expect) are actually good for the mental health of employees.

One emotional aspect of the quality of everyday life most profoundly affected by work, and by the technology of work, may be the so-called "work–life balance," since sources of happiness such as partners or family, holidays or hobbies, are exactly the "drag-coefficients" that were explicitly — at least in the above instance referred to by Arlie Russell Hochschild — unfavourable to employers.

Sociologist Judy Wajcman (2015) has argued that, precisely because of how technology serves capitalism, the increased dependency on technology to mediate aspects of our lives has mostly added to a sense of what she calls *temporal impoverishment*, rather than making us more efficient and thus freeing us up to enjoy more of our lives. More interestingly, this is the case across lines of class, even if the experiences of time impoverishment are different. "The key to understanding the fraught and complex relationship between technology and time is the concept of temporal sovereignty, the ability to choose how you spend your time," Wajcman says. Time sovereignty, she argues, is a matter of social justice, and is "a significant measure of life satisfaction and well-being."

When the work–life balance tips too far in favour of satisfying the requirements of work, family life suffers, and the toll is emotional. In her other work, Hochschild (1997) has found from interviewing working parents that the importance of home life decreases as professional level increases, and the direct tension between them is reminiscent of the parents working at Sports Direct who are so scared of losing their jobs that they neglect aspects of their children's lives. As psychologist Oliver James has found in his book *Selfish Capitalism*, it is a feature of capitalism that children receive less attention from their parents, causing emotional damage to the children as well as the parents (2008).

Another source of wellbeing cut down by time poverty is sleep. As Jonathan Crary (2013) has written, capitalism frequently demands that we sleep less than we need to. It is common for people to "humble brag" about how little sleep they get by on, and perhaps it is no surprise that British ex-prime minister Margaret Thatcher was said to get only four hours per night during her heyday of wrecking Britain. Sleep deprivation has been linked to immune-system suppression, weight gain, and psychiatric distress. Sleep deprivation also makes people far more emotionally vulnerable. In a study by psychologist Matthew Walker at the University of California, Berkeley, test subjects who had gone thirty-five hours without sleep had a far stronger response to mildly distressing images, such as those of burn victims, than test subjects who had slept. An article on the study in *Scientific American* reports that:

> In normal participants, the amygdala seemed to be talking to the medial prefrontal cortex, an outer layer of the brain that, Walker says, helps to contextualize experiences and emotions. But, in the sleep-deprived brain, the amygdala seemed to be "rewired," coupling instead with a brain stem area called the locus coeruleus, which secretes norepinephrine, a precursor of the hormone adrenaline that triggers fight-or-flight type reactions.

Taken together, what these issues underline is that where people are faced with a choice between undermining their financial survival or undermining their personal and emotional wellbeing, people seem to be choosing the latter. This is indicative not only of growing desperation and precarity, but of a culture in which emotions are often not explicitly valued; we are expected to "handle it," to "be strong," or to "pull an all-nighter," while the emotional pressures we experience slowly intensify.

In his *Economic and Philosophic Manuscripts of 1844*, Karl Marx wrote of the concept of *alienation*. Alienation is a far broader and more multifaceted philosophical concept here than in his subsequent works, but is used to mean the variety of ways in which the relations entailed in labour affect the emotional reality of the worker. Workers being considered only as a cost, for instance, rather than as people, has implications for how they are treated in the workplace, and thus for their emotions. Shouting at employees over a PA system to work harder and faster, for example (as mocked in the Daft Punk song), is like something out of a dystopian film, yet it is exactly what happens at Sports Direct, according to the report mentioned above. The fact that the things we make, or the services we provide, even when doing something as important as educating people, are immediately claimed as the product or service of our employer is also a form of alienation. Whether from passion or from fear, it is not hard to see how putting everything into doing your job as best you can, only to find that the output of this labour belongs entirely to the same employer that is reducing or deferring your pay and treating you like a layabout or a common thief, would be emotionally taxing. Working such long hours or unusual shifts that you do not see your family or friends, or are not home for your children when they return from school, alienates you from the important people in your life. All of these are different aspects of alienation, and what is important about this concept for our purposes is precisely that the various effects of being a worker are acknowledged to all go beyond the material circumstances of the worker and also impact the individual in an emotionally significant way. Ron Roberts has gone so far as to argue that alienation is a far better concept for understanding the common emotional experiences of life under capitalism than anything in the American Psychiatric Association's *Diagnostic and Statistical Manual of Mental Disorders* or DSM. It is getting easier by the day to see what he means.

For those who seek to love their work, the pressures and uncertainty referred to above are not much better, especially for younger people. In an article for openDemocracy, Angela McRobbie (2015) outlined the alarming process by which recent graduates, determined to work in the so-called "creative industries," are happy to be exploited by low pay and long hours in the belief that this will lead to a glamorous professional life working creatively in fashion or the media. Somewhat ironically, perhaps their insistence on "creative labour" is indicative of the emotional distress they perceive to be likely should they perform less creative forms of labour. In some sense, they would be right; creativity entails a connection with the work you produce that in capitalism is broken by the process of alienation. As soon as the work is finished it is not your work anymore, you will receive no credit, and now you have to move onto the next task which will culminate in exactly the same outcome. Some young people do receive credit and plaudits but it is rare, as I have seen teaching passionate young journalists. Assuming they can even get a job, they usually take a few more years before they get a "byline," or their name at the top of an article. Creative labour for "the man" is as alienated as any other form of labour, and unfortunately, is far from guaranteed to be as enjoyable as expected.

Distinct from the alienation of Marx, German critical theorist Herbert Marcuse spoke of an artistic alienation, born of making "romantic" artistic work in a society that is at odds with the truth that the art expresses; but my young students, and those referred to by McRobbie, are alienated in yet another way: Rather than expressing themselves, or some otherwise inexpressible truth, they want to do creative work that is almost entirely in keeping with the dominant values of society. This is entirely understandable given the cultural pressures to which they are subjected, but what makes it a different form of alienation is the desperation to do creative work that is more about where they, as the creators of such work, belong in that society as a consequence. The desire to be publicly credited for your work in glamorous areas such fashion, music, advertising, or design is therefore not solely a desire to avoid the emotional distress and boredom of other forms of labour. In an age where most young people want to be famous, it often represents a highly individualised form of upward social mobility as well, and this is a reflection of wider issues that also come into play emotionally.

What is Instagram, but the ability to share an image with a caption to "followers"? Mechanically it is little more, but while its users have made it into a platform of many uses, one of its chief uses is for those looking to become famous. From food bloggers to photographers to musicians to models, the idea is the same: Show who you are and what you can do to enough people and the rest will happen. Do a search for "how to get famous on Instagram" and you will find pages of blog posts and videos, all without a hint of irony, offering tips on how to "get popular," "make it," or at least "get more likes." Here, as so often with social media, we see that a platform launched speculatively is being carried by the specific cultural uses that its users bring to it; and that technologies are a reflection of the cultures in which they are used, rather than determinant of those cultures.

The widespread desire to be famous, especially amongst the young, could be interpreted as an inverse manifestation of exactly the emotional fragility that is entailed in daily life. It is the hyper-valuation of what has been called the "personal brand"; your name, your appearance and body, and/or the work you are known for (if any). To be famous is imagined to be constant validation and adoration, financial security, ample sociality, unalienated, creative work, and the means to afford regular novelty and stimulation. From appearance to self-worth to talent to the very fact of having a future at all, fame appears to be a means to avoid every fear that a young person might have, all at once. Intense identification with famous people, seen in magazines like *Heat*, in programs like *The X Factor*, or in the *Daily Mail*'s "sidebar of shame," is precisely because of the "lucky escape" that these individuals have managed. Of course, while the desire to be famous is itself mainstream, the precise form that fame is imagined to take need not always be the same, and can vary widely with class and background; but the function of fame as a fantasy is the same — it is a coping method. Reading fame as such therefore allows us to identify a number of other areas of postmodern life that are fraught with emotional distress, or the potential for it, and not just for the young.

The irony here is that the pressure to have a "personal brand," rather than a means of security and stability, is a way in which the emotional toll of postmodern culture can be intensified, and its pressures increased. Even for those less interested in fame itself, the same culture of intense individual evaluation in every area of life does not evaporate. Even the search for what else might have been written about the idea of the personal brand is instructive: Besides countless blog posts, what seem like hundreds of scholarly articles unreservedly promise to provide insight on the various uses of personal branding, while the more cautious voices are rather harder to find. It seems the desire to be famous is not just a young people's thing after all. From an article by three academics at the University of Utah in 2005, I learn that the idea of the personal brand was coined in 1997, the same year that Silicon Valley was going on about "drag coefficients."

One of the most important changes to have taken place in the culture of capitalism is the incorporation of the economic logic of capitalism into all areas of life, inside and outside the workplace. Often, the term used for this scenario is *neoliberalism*, and the idea of it is that market logic should be the only logic for assessing value. Political scientist Wendy Brown has summarised this tendency well. In neoliberalism, she says, "all conduct is economic conduct; all spheres of existence are framed and measured by economic terms

and metrics, even when those spheres are not directly monetized"
(2015). In a similar vein, writer George Monbiot has said that
"Neoliberalism sees competition as the defining characteristic of
human relations. […] It maintains that 'the market' delivers benefits
that could never be achieved by planning" (2016b). Neoliberalism is
UK supermarket Waitrose forcing the charities it supports to *compete*
with each other for a greater proportion of funds, by appealing to
the public to place little green tokens in one box or another; it is the
obsessive comparison of the percentage of completed passes or goals
per game in football, instead of focusing on questions of playing style;
it is the insistence that university lecturers be rated by students on
how enthusiastic they are about the subject matter they teach.

People often hear the word "neoliberalism" as a catch-all stick
with which to moan about capitalism, but its effects are serious
and numerous. The obsession of (some of) my students with their
grades, for example, is no longer a healthy desire for brief feedback
and then self-improvement; it is treated as an evaluation of who
they are, often with frantic results. It frequently feels like marking a
student essay in the neoliberal age is seen as more akin to assigning
an Uber driver a rating out of five stars for their service, or swiping
left or right on Tinder, than providing a person who is being educated
with information about how well they are undertaking that process.
It is hardly surprising that student feedback has been subsumed by
neoliberalism in this way; the idea that we are all measurable, and all
in competition with each other on the basis of these measurements,
is widely accepted, and superficial measures of quantification and
assessment are easy to spot.

As disturbingly portrayed by UK comedian Charlie Brooker in
the 2016 series *Black Mirror*, the quantification, rating, ranking,
and scoring of individual human beings, while of cultural origins,
is further enabled and amplified by networked, digital technology.
Klout, a so-called "social media analytics service" promises to
evaluate how authoritative you are overall in your online social-

network usage, assigning you a single number from one to a hundred known as your "Klout score." The platform uses data from Facebook, Twitter, YouTube, Instagram, and other platforms, essentially to determine your *value*. The logical extension of this would be the idea that your very worth as a person is quantified, and in 2015, despite a major backlash, a service called Peeple was launched that would allow people to rate you generally as a person. In 2014, a supposedly "alternative" artist known as MLV even created a set of downloadable stencils that would allow graffiti artists to leave rankings and ratings on their physical environment, such as bathroom stalls and water fountains, seemingly without seeing the need to subvert this way of thinking at all.

The quantification of "friends," as a cornerstone of social networks, and most notably Facebook, is an especially interesting imprint of this culture of quantification. How many friends do *you* have? Most people know, but pretend not to. It is understandable that social networks allow us to connect socially — and as we will see in the next chapter, it is essential to their strategy — but specifically the quantification of friends, and the overt display of this information on every user's profile, is an opportunity to observe one of the many ironies of this culture as a whole. Despite the average woman having 164 friends on Facebook at the time of writing, and the average man having 144, most people would turn to no more than five individuals for support (Dunbar, 2016). What this may confirm is that such personal quantifications are, like much of the digital self, often performative, and do not tell the whole story. When credit ratings, grades, Airbnb ratings, TripAdvisor ratings and reviews, "friend," "follower," and "likes" counts, and even the secret attractiveness ratings that services such as Tinder and Clover calculate about you are taken into account, and when competition on this basis is constantly affirmed and demanded, it is hardly surprising that neoliberalism places enormous individual emotional strain on those exposed to its workings. Whether or not you are invested in getting good grades, rankings, or ratings, being constantly evaluated in very narrow terms is not psychologically healthy, yet this is everywhere in our culture. By quantifying aspects of who you are that are not in any way quantitative and that cannot justly be represented by a number, it adds pressure precisely in areas where we are most vulnerable. Obsessive focus on individual performance objectifies and commodifies the self in the same way that society encourages the objectification of others. Experiencing yourself as a commodity alienates you from yourself — yet another form of the alienation Marx described. Such metrics are also frequently a means of comparison to people with whom competition is wholly unfair; the people society has made richer, decided are hotter, more intelligent, or more talented.

Loneliness, boredom and materialism

Whatever the frenzy of online social connection, with friend counts soaring, many people are nevertheless lonely and socially isolated. Adding friends on Facebook may be a futile attempt at compensation for some degree of social isolation, rather than an affirmation or retrenchment of existing social networks. The continuity between the neoliberal quantification of social capital on social networks and the social isolation of neoliberalism is more than coincidence. As George Monbiot has remarked: "Perhaps it's unsurprising that Britain, in which neoliberal ideology has been most rigorously applied, is the loneliness capital of Europe. We are all neoliberals now" (2016b). According to *Loneliness* by neuroscientists John Cacioppo and William Patrick (2009), "roughly twenty percent of individuals — that would be sixty million people in the U.S. alone — feel sufficiently isolated for it to be a major source of unhappiness in their lives." Later on, they write that over the last five decades especially, "Western societies have demoted human gregariousness from a necessity to an incidental." The steady transition from rural to urban living that has accompanied both industrialisation and then the subsequent transition to the postmodern world is also linked with social isolation. Oliver James (2008) has gone so far as to demonstrate the role of this urbanisation in greatly exacerbating more extreme forms of emotional distress and mental illness such as schizophrenia. San Francisco journalist Lauren Smiley wrote in 2015 of what she called the "shut-in economy": Socially isolated people, working from home in luxury San Francisco apartments, ordering everything to their door from the internet, including meals. Perhaps it isn't just the Amazon or UberEATS employees who are miserable — it would seem as if their customers are too. Could the very popularity of such businesses be related to urbanised social isolation? Isn't the whole point of ordering a meal or a book or a new gadget from the internet and having it brought to your door that no human contact is required? Of course, if society were lonely, wouldn't people seek the human contact replaced by such affordances? Not necessarily. It is more likely that the same processes of social isolation in the city produce the shut-ins, the loneliness, and the schizophrenia.

One of the aspects of postmodern life that Oliver James identifies as particularly conducive to poor emotional wellbeing is materialism. Specifically, James refers to what he calls "relative materialism" — the kind of materialism that occurs when people already have necessities such as food, shelter, adequate drinking water and a means of subsistence. Relying heavily on the work of psychologist Erich Fromm, and echoing Marx, James argues that by living to *have*, rather than living to *be*, people set themselves up for anxiety and boredom, because material possessions are not, and cannot be, emotionally fulfilling. Expecting them to be, in the ways that consumerism encourages, means constantly mismatched expectations. A new car, new laptop, new dress may make us feel happy momentarily, but there is a big difference between hedonic happiness, associated with pleasure, and long-term fulfilment, known as *eudaimonic* happiness. The hedonic pleasure and the feelings of pride from the novelty of obtaining some shiny new possession invariably subside, and if eudaimonic happiness was missing before, it will still be missing. Over time, the repeated experience of getting used to a new product and going back to the same life you had before is one that, if you expect products to make you happy, even subconsciously, will make you feel emptier than ever. As author Alfie Bown (2015) has written, capitalist culture emphasises the aspects of itself that are there to be enjoyed, be they a Netflix series, stuffed-crust pizza, Pokémon Go, or a cruise holiday. But many people are constantly left behind by this emphasis on material or hedonic comfort, unable to afford the enjoyment in which they are subtly told they must participate. Even if the *having* of the hedonic pleasures afforded to some of us will not make us happy, the constant feeling of *not having* — of missing out — will also build anger, resentment, and a feeling of injustice, that all take their toll. Psychologist Barry Schwartz has also famously shown the emotional toll of choice. Beyond a certain threshold, the greater our expectations and the number of options we can choose between, the less satisfied we are with our choice.

Connected with consumerism, boredom is another widespread and distressing feature of capitalist life. Sociologist Zygmunt Bauman noted in *Consuming Life* that

> for the properly trained members of the society of consumers, all and any routine and everything associated with routine behaviour (monotony, repetitiveness) becomes unbearable; indeed, unliveable. "Boredom", the absence or even temporary interruption of the perpetual flow of attention-drawing, exciting novelties, turns into a resented and feared bugbear of the consumer society. (2007)

The problem of how workers can be kept working and prevented from becoming bored is one of capitalism's oldest problems, and as we will see it is directly connected to the use of social media alongside other subjective and emotional distress. People experience boredom to varying degrees, but anyone who is chronically unstimulated or whose life consists of too much monotony, whether from work, poverty, materialism, or otherwise, will be well acquainted with boredom. Many forms of work are boring, from working in a call centre to marking pile after pile of essays to helping customers try on clothes that neither they nor you can actually afford. As a crippling symptom of many societies in its own right, boredom also has a range of other emotional effects. According to science journalist Anna Gosline, "Easily bored people are at higher risk for depression, anxiety, drug addiction, alcoholism, compulsive gambling, eating disorders, hostility, anger, poor social skills, bad grades and low work performance" (2007). Alongside alienation, the fear and uncertainty that come from precarity, and social isolation, boredom is at epidemic levels, largely because — as we will see below — we look in the wrong places for the solutions.

Late capitalism as a culture of emotional distress

Lest this long list of ways people commonly experience emotional distress in so-called modern life appears to be nothing more than me looking for things that make people unhappy, let me clarify: This is exactly what it is. And such elements to life are easier than ever to find and identify. We do not all need to agree with, or have experienced, all of the issues outlined above, but almost all of us will have experienced some of them.

There is something else that all these factors in our emotional distress have in common too, as may have already become obvious. All of the forms of emotional distress described above are derived from aspects of how capitalism now operates. When aspects of capitalism are remarked upon, these arguments are often heard by those unused to such critiques, as if capitalism were only an economic system. To criticise capitalism in this light is therefore to pose it in relation to other economic and political situations such as communism in its various historical forms, feudalism possibly, or the plain old "state of nature" in which philosophers such as Thomas Hobbes, John Locke, and others imagined our ancestors living. Since these alternative economic systems to capitalism are at this point mostly historical, thinking of capitalism as though it were purely an economic system also tends to mean hearing such critiques of it as though they were a desire to return to these historical states that preceded it. Familiar and simplistic arguments are then rehearsed about the numerous shortcomings of Maoist China or the Soviet Union, after which another "alternative" is demanded.

Such arguments are a distraction, because capitalism is not only an abstract set of rules about how to organise an economy, or a way to make money. Indeed, when only these aspects of capitalism are present, many of the problems to be described below disappear. To give one example, two close friends of mine run a business in a small English city, employing approximately twenty-five people and turning over something not far short of a million pounds per year. They provide their staff not only with generous pay, but with a wide variety of perks and surprises, ample (and equal) maternity and paternity leave, paid holiday far in excess of the statutory minimums, and opportunities for training, development, and promotion. Business ideas suggested by workers are often incorporated into the workings of the company, and so far as possible employees are given the maximum degree of autonomy in how they fulfil their duties. The business has a strict code of ethics, reduces its ecological impact in every area from transport to energy consumption to recycling, and sponsors a number of community initiatives, particularly around young people at the nearby university. However far to the left you are, this is one version of capitalism that, on a practical basis at least, it is difficult to criticise. It is an example of what psychologist Oliver James (2008) calls "unselfish capitalism." Of course in a Marxist sense these workers are still technically "exploited," and the business does still make a profit from such exploitation, so there is no doubt that this is still "capitalism." But while these may still be doctrinal problems, even if their effects are ameliorated away to nothing, the pedantic arguments that plague the left in respect of these philosophical problems in the abstract are arguably a hindrance to the establishment of exactly the proletarian unity that Marx urged. All of the people working for this company are as vulnerable to capitalism as any other individuals, yet ironically, this vulnerability is not to be found so much at their current workplace as outside of it. The "capitalism" that must be addressed in relation to social media is therefore one that operates at a far broader scale — that of society itself.

To achieve its ultimate ends, capitalism must be the culture of those that live under it. Rather than rehearsing the arguments of critical philosophers in this area such as Louis Althusser, Fredric Jameson, or Stuart Hall, let it suffice to say that even if capitalism began as an economic system that was imposed on the world by those who had the power and inclination to do so, capitalism is now a culture that determines how our society should work, rather than the other way around. If there occurs some aspect of how corporations conduct their affairs that deserves critique, such as sub-prime lending, children mining tin from the ground to make components for iPhones, or the extraction of vast profits from selling arms to murderous world leaders, these kinds of workings within what is more conspicuously identifiable as the capitalist system are simply the manifestations of the *culture* of capitalism, rather than the reverse. The same is true of the ways that our emotional distress is implicated in capitalism: It is the product of capitalism as culture.

At risk of deploying "capitalism" as some sort of fixed, structuralist signifier — a uniform source of all economic and social ills — it should be noted that capitalism is not one fixed, inflexible system. The subjective experience of life in capitalist culture is different for each person, and exactly where capitalism begins and ends is by no means stable or certain. Even when only its economic logic is discussed, its workings are subject to constant and often radical change. However, the very point of identifying capitalist economics and capitalist culture as one inseparable and ultimately cultural system is precisely that we can better understand the radical, constantly changing nature of capitalism, and adapt our critiques to the forms that it assumes, especially in relation to what else is happening in the world at any given time. The capitalism of the 1950s and 1960s, for example, was different to the postmodern form under which we live today in at least one important respect: While as an economic framework capitalism is the only system on offer today, capitalism in 1960 had to contend with what were considered rival systems — chiefly communism. Despite many shortcomings, it had to be something that people would prefer to be included in over communism. The emphasis of this capitalism was modernity: Space programs, electric guitars, cars with fins on them, new types of food from novel production processes or from faraway exotic places. Of course, there were exploited, alienated workers, unemployment, and poverty in this capitalism too, since capitalism needs these elements to exist, but the *cultural life* of this capitalism was very different. After the end of the Soviet Union, and particularly once Margaret Thatcher and Ronald Reagan ushered in their distinctive form of free-market economics, the culture of capitalist societies began to change too. Perhaps one could say it changed from a capitalism that was functional in some way to one that is not, or maybe this is too simple; but it did change from a capitalism that did not produce as much emotional distress to one that does rather more, and for reasons that we will see below, eventually from a capitalism that didn't have — or need — social media, to one that does.

This change from a capitalism that needed on some level to prove its legitimacy with modernism and innovation to a capitalism that did not is often called *late capitalism* or *postmodernity*, and has been widely remarked upon. Political scientist Francis Fukuyama famously referred to this moment as the "end of history," but it was more the end of the future. Once capitalism as a system of economics, politics, and culture was without any alternatives, the role of politics in imagining or fighting for the future began to change. As Adam Curtis has said in his 2016 film *HyperNormalisation*, the end of the Soviet Union "symbolised the final failure of the dream that politics could be used to build a new kind of world." Whatever we may think of the "end-of-history" idea, the change had significant cultural impact. Mark Fisher, building on the work of various philosophers, most of all Fredric Jameson, has argued powerfully for an understanding of this postmodern, late capitalism as being defined precisely by its feeling of there being "no alternative," as Margaret Thatcher's Conservative Party repeatedly said during the 1980s. Fisher calls this "capitalist realism." After the fall of the Berlin Wall, he says, "Fukuyama's thesis that history has climaxed with liberal capitalism may have been widely derided, but is accepted, even assumed, at the level of the cultural unconscious."

This change has had far-reaching cultural, and eventually emotional, consequences. Most famously, Fredric Jameson identified "postmodernism" (as distinct from the broader historical era, known as *postmodernity*) as the ways in which this change to late capitalism was inflected at the cultural level. The invention of new styles in art and other forms of culture had become impossible at this point, he argued:

In an era in which stylistic innovation is no longer possible, all that is left is to imitate dead styles, to speak through the masks and with the voices of the styles in the imaginary museum. But this means that contemporary or postmodernist art is going to be about art itself in a new kind of way; even more, it means that one of its essential messages will involve the necessary failure of art and the aesthetic, the failure of the new, the imprisonment in the past.

There are many things that have been or can be said about this moment, and reading both Jameson's and Fisher's work is highly recommended, but for present purposes one of the most important strands is in Fisher's concept of capitalist realism, outlined above. Here we are interested in emotion and psychology, and capitalist realism is significant in a discussion of social media because it recognises the mental-health impact of living in an intensified capitalist culture from which there is no escape besides temporary distraction.

The potency of this feeling of no escape has been well illustrated in the popularity of politicians such as Bernie Sanders and Jeremy Corbyn. Both have captured the imagination of millions of people because, particularly in Corbyn's case, they were able to articulate a vision of a country or even a world *outside* capitalist realism. While people may not have been consciously aware of their hunger for an alternative, as soon as one was dangled, its resonance was immediate and entirely predictable. Equally predictable was how the establishment in the countries of both men — the guardians of the capitalist realism — immediately attacked them for being "unelectable," of all things. The press, largely the subservient watchdogs of capitalist realism, for the most part also undermined these candidates.

In a political context, Mark Fisher outlines convincingly the relationship between political agency and capitalist realism with what he calls "reflexive impotence." Fisher argues that the political disengagement of British students, for example, is because "they know things are bad, but more than that, they know they can't do anything about it. But that 'knowledge', that reflexivity, is not a passive observation of an already-existing state of affairs. It is a self-fulfilling prophecy." A year after Fisher's book came out, British students did fight back, to fight the controversial rise in tuition fees announced by the then-newly-elected coalition government. What happened? Thousands and thousands of young people were kettled by the police — imprisoned in the cold and dark for hours. They were mocked in virtually all the newspapers. Most of all, their pleas for change and for inclusion in the political process were completely ignored, no doubt confirming the reflexive impotence of the students who have followed, paying the higher tuition fees.

If you believe that nobody listens to you, including the people for
whom you have voted, that you have no clear future over which you
are in control, and that nothing you do will make difference, what is
your next step? Detailing the emotional impact on young people by
recounting his experiences of teaching in a further-education college
in London, Mark Fisher tells us that: "Many of the teenagers I worked
with had mental health problems or learning difficulties. Depression
is endemic." In July 2016 James Meikle reported in the *Guardian*
that prescriptions for antidepressants in England had doubled in a
decade. According to a study by the UK's National Health Service and
the University of Leicester, reported in the *Guardian*, "between 1993
and 2014 there was a 35% rise in adults reporting severe symptoms
of common mental disorders." These symptoms are more acute in
younger people, and particularly in women. An enormous 26% of
women aged eighteen to twenty-four reported having had symptoms
of common mental disorders in the previous week (Campbell &
Siddique, 2016). As George Monbiot (2016a) has asked: "Is it any
wonder, in these lonely inner worlds, in which touching has been
replaced by retouching, that young women are drowning in mental
distress?" Mark Fisher tells us that "Being a teenager in late capitalist
Britain is now close to being reclassified as a sickness." He continues:

> This pathologisation already forecloses any possibility of
> politicisation. By privatising these problems – treating them as if
> they were caused only by chemical imbalances in the individual's
> neurology and/or by their family background – any question of
> social systemic causation is ruled out.

Indeed, Ron Roberts argues that the very purpose of psychiatry
as a science has its roots in serving the ruling class by diagnosing
and then controlling those who stepped out of line, and is thus not
likely to help us draw political connections with psychiatric issues.
Psychologist Oliver James similarly takes issue with the notion that

emotional distress is caused solely by private or personal factors such as genetics, arguing that it is far more likely to be caused by environmental factors.

Filling the void

Now that we have seen some of these environmental factors — anxiety, boredom, loneliness, and depression — and their environmental causes within the broader society of labour, disenfranchisement, materialism, and so forth, the question becomes: How do they play out? This brings us back to the compensatory patterns outlined in Chapter Two.

Mark Fisher makes a very important point about how his students behave, and introduces the concept of *depressive hedonia*. "Depression is usually characterised as a state of anhedonia," he writes, but depressive hedonia

is constituted not by an inability to get pleasure, so much as by an inability to do anything else *except* pursue pleasure. There is a sense that "something is missing," but no appreciation that this mysterious, missing enjoyment can only be accessed *beyond* the pleasure principle.

The importance of the concept of depressive hedonia cannot be overstated for the purposes of comprehending social media in the way I believe is necessary. Having outlined the compulsive, pleasure-seeking, and above all emotionally driven nature of social media in the previous chapter, and hinted at the compensatory role that social media may provide, it is now possible to argue more explicitly how that pattern fits within a broader emotional and cultural landscape. As in the Louis CK quote at the beginning of this chapter, there are reasons to feel empty almost as soon as you are conscious of your own existence, but as we have seen above, there are a myriad of ways that the emotional pressures of life in a late-capitalist consumer society add to this. When these forms of emotional distress combine, like bright colours mixing to become brown, our sense of exactly what we are feeling, or why, is often unclear. Instead, the common sentiment is simply a feeling of unexplained emptiness and tension; a dull malaise. The worst part about its indistinctive, bland character is that while the feeling may be strong, it does not clearly push in one direction or another, and this is why the "something" that is missing is mysterious. As with many forms of emotional distress, sometimes we may deny to ourselves and to others that we feel bad at all. Psychologist Erich Fromm also observed this, asking: "Are people really happy, are they as satisfied, unconsciously, as they believe themselves to be? Considering the nature of man, and the conditions for happiness, this can hardly be so."

This sense of an ill-defined unease which has no name or clear origin, and may not even be consciously realised at all, but which can be temporarily satisfied and remedied with hedonic activity, is an old theme that has been recognised in a number of other contexts that are helpful for understanding social media. One encapsulation of this idea is in the German adjective *ersatz*, meaning the inferiority of a replacement. An *ersatz* experience is chosen because it is the closest option to replace some superior, but unavailable experience. Along similar lines, French psychoanalyst Jacques Lacan wrote of the concept of "*l'objet petit a*," something constantly sought after and desired, but which can never be obtained and enjoyed. For Lacan, this feeling was an intrinsic quality of how humans are motivated to relate to and desire aspects of their environs, originating deep in their psychological development, rather than something precipitated primarily by external cultural circumstances like those described above. Nevertheless, so far as the social media timeline is a consumption architecture, and consumption is — as sociologist Zygmunt Bauman has argued (2001) — driven by desire, the concept is still very much applicable.

The distinct notions of *ersatz*, *l'objet petit a*, and depressive hedonia all provide valuable, overlapping insights into the psychology of compulsive social media use, and the role social media play when, as Mark Fisher says, "something is missing". When taken together, the emotional distress of life under capitalism, the *ersatz* compensatory role of hedonic media consumption, and the consumption-centric orientation of social media reveal that that compulsive social media use is driven by the desire to soothe and to be distracted from the generalised emotional distress and malaise of everyday late-capitalist life. I refer to this behaviour as *filling the void*.

The generalised malaise of late capitalist life has therefore been met by social media's promise of a generalised solution. But it is a cruel, unkept promise, and an ineffective solution. We are seeking that "something" to make us feel better in a place we will never find it. As much as social media may be "hedonic" while a user consumes them, they cease to provide any lasting benefit from the moment the session finishes, and ironically can even make users feel worse — more unhappy from moment to moment and more dissatisfied with their lives generally (Kross et al., 2013). Ultimately, all they can provide is distraction. This harsh irony typifies a circularity that is essential to the workings of consumerism. As we have seen in this chapter, the experience of late capitalism appears to be implicated in making its subjects miserable. Yet within that system of capitalism, specific enterprises also derive wealth and value from promising temporary reprieve from this exact same emotional distress, even if they have no effect or make things worse overall. When, as with social media, the solutions on offer feel pleasurable at the moment they are consumed, consumers fail to identify when these ineffective solutions have the result of making them feel worse, meaning they have no problem going back for more.

James Davies (2011) has argued that what he calls "negative models of suffering" turn our emotional distress into something that must be treated and anaesthetised, in a way that is ultimately "socially and individually disadvantageous." For any industry that is looking to sell us solutions, however, this desire to anaesthetise our distress is highly advantageous. One industry has harvested gains more proximate to our misery than any other: the pharmaceutical industry. The enormous growth in the prescription of antidepressants, referred to above, is not simply an indicator of a corresponding growth in depression and anxiety; it is also a major business opportunity, despite the evidence of their effectiveness being mixed at best, and many traditional SSRI drugs such as Citalopram often causing intolerable side effects (Drugs.com, 2000). A study from 2006, before the most recent explosion in antidepressant use, showed that 56% of the three hundred panel members who oversee the American Psychological Association's *Diagnostic and Statistical Manual of Mental Disorders* (DSM-IV) had financial interests in the pharmaceutical industry, and recommended greater transparency (Cosgrove et al, 2006).

But there are also other ways the markets can end up appearing to be the solution to our unhappiness, and in one way or another this has been a part of how capitalism has worked for decades. As management scholar Mats Alvesson reminds us, increased consumption "is paralleled by a continual growth in demand without any increase in satisfaction" (2013). The founder of cosmetics chain Revlon, Charles Revson, once reportedly said that "In our factory we make cosmetics. In the store we sell hope." Communicated in this sinister phrase is an understanding that people who are starved of fulfilment or hope will give you anything if you make them feel hopeful again. As any drug dealer knows, the same is true of pleasure, even if the costs and drawbacks are high. The basic premise of consumerism is to confuse one with the other. If people are unhappy, insecure, disenfranchised, lonely, horny, or whatever it may be, you can sell them things far more easily, even if these "solutions" are anything but. The combination of emotionally distressing features of postmodern, late-capitalist life that I have outlined above makes for very fertile ground to do exactly this.

Versions of this pattern exist everywhere. In capitalism's search to extract surplus value from anywhere it can be found, the market has long claimed legitimacy in the right to sell us hedonic or addictive things that aren't good for us. Many of the hedonic pleasures described in Chapter Two, such as tobacco, sugar, and junk food, have been part of this pattern. Businesses such as UberEATS, Deliveroo, and Just Eat in the UK, and US equivalents such as Grubhub and Delivery.com, exist solely for the purpose of bringing you food from restaurants. They seem like a mere practical service until we recall that most people who can afford to use these services are not starving, and are capable of cooking food themselves. Such businesses derive their value from delivering more enjoyable, hedonic food. According to research carried out for HBO's *Last Week Tonight with John Oliver*, sugar is a five-billion-dollar industry, and the average US American consumes 75 lbs (34 kg) of sugar every year. As Sanjida O'Connell has shown in her book *Sugar: The Grass that Changed the World*, sugar can give you an emotional "buzz" from dopamine and serotonin. Some researchers, such as David Ludwig, argue sugar affects the brain in the same way as street drugs such as heroin or cocaine. O'Connell quotes neuroscientist Candace Pert, who states that: "I consider sugar to be a drug, a highly purified plant product that can become addictive. Relying on an artificial form of glucose — sugar — to give us a quick pick-me-up is analogous to, if not as dangerous as, shooting heroin." A 1969 industry ad for sugar in *Time* magazine even proclaimed: "If sugar can fill that hollow feeling, I'm all for it." Sound familiar?

Facebook, Twitter, and Instagram may be free, but they are still corporations that make money from your using them. Whatever their original form, they have evolved to encircle and exploit the unhappiness of capitalist subjects while providing them with depressive hedonia in the form of the timeline. Emotions, once considered worthless, have now become a site at which value can be mercilessly extracted for commercial gain. As social media incorporate themselves ever deeper and into more intimate aspects of our lives, they become the fastest, cheapest way of *filling the void*, and it is their strategy to do exactly this to which the next chapter turns.

— FOUR —

You are now "in a relationship"

For the love of money
People will steal from their mother,
For the love of money
People will rob their own brother,
For the love of money
People can't even walk the street
Because they never know who in the world they're gonna beat,
For that lean, mean, mean green
Almighty dollar, money.

The O'Jays

The price of anything is the amount of life you exchange for it.

Henry David Thoreau

They "trust me," dumb fucks.

Mark Zuckerberg, Facebook CEO,
speaking about early Facebook users

We get it all the time.

Sergeant Brink, LA Police Department, on people calling
the police for help when Facebook is unavailable

This book has so far focused on our consumptive use of social media, emphasising what we get from that usage, what our motivations are for seeking those rewards, and the emotional and cultural contexts in which that consumption takes place. To acknowledge the enjoyment in any act of consumption, however, is not to ascribe unqualified positive value to it. Understanding consumption, including that of timeline media, is essential, but it would not be a complete picture without looking at the broader commercial and economic paradigm within which our "filling" of the "void" takes place. Consumption is part of an exchange, and for all that we might get from our use of social media, or hope that we'll get from them each time we open a particular social media app or website, the large companies that own these platforms get a great deal from us too. We need to examine the terms of that exchange very carefully, and it is against this backdrop that we must understand why the idea of "filling the void" matters so much. It is to the nature of this exchange that this chapter turns.

Hiding in plain sight

One of the most important foundations of Marx's critiques of capitalism was his view of all economics as being based on relationships. Both in the context of social media and in consumerism generally, this emphasis on relationships is uncommon beyond academic and activist circles, but it can be very useful to help us understand the nature of the relationships that our ongoing exchanges with social media corporations — like with any other corporations — comprise.

Much bigger questions have been asked about how social media platforms mediate our relationship with government than about how they might our relationship with capital. Your relationship with the state is an explicit, conspicuous one that has always been and should always remain subject to constant contestation and struggle. You know you are a taxpayer, that you can vote, that you have to follow the speed limit, that you may have to serve on a jury, and in some countries, that your government has the authority to decide whether you live or die. The power it holds is supposed to be exercised in your name as a citizen, and any other exercise of it is considered a distortion of the democratic system. Such distortions are both common and predictable, and it's not hard to see why we might not trust governments. Meanwhile, as powerful as many corporations are to affect your life in various ways, you might never know it. Our relationships with capital are often far more hidden than those we have with the state, and this difference extends onto social media.

The debate around social media as they relate to structures of power has similarly been characterised by a focus on government. To begin with, this discussion consisted of techno-utopian excitement that social media might somehow comprise an effective, yet peaceful, weapon against the state, as relationship to power was applied to the then-new technology. Thankfully, these rather naïve proclamations have largely been put to bed by the insistent polemics of Evgeny Morozov (2011) and others. The revelations made by Edward Snowden in June 2013 put the final nail in the coffin of the once-popular wishful thinking about Twitter and Facebook revolutions. Even more important than bringing a degree of realism to how technology relates to conspicuous forms of power such as government is to look elsewhere for relationships with power that are mediated by technology. But there has been far less discussion of how our use of social media platforms might comprise direct relationships with large, often publicly-listed corporations. What was most damning about the classified documents that Edward Snowden made available to the world was precisely the way that information we had been quite happy to give away to private capital had found its way into the hands of governments, but it was the governments who bore the brunt of public outcry. But while there has been a documented "chilling effect" in how people search the web and use Wikipedia after these revelations (Penney, 2016), there is no research to show any significant effects on the use of social media, or of Apple, Microsoft, and Google products. Most of the people who talk about social media in the context of our relationships with capital are "social media gurus" who sell their knowledge of how people use social media to help earn their client companies more money. But why are we so much more trusting of large corporations with exactly the same information that we know we don't want governments to have? If you have a problem about the government knowing where you are at all times, why tell Facebook where you are every time you use the app?

The answer to these questions is probably that our economic relationships, especially with larger corporations, are usually far less conspicuous, and most people are far less accustomed to an adversarial relationship with capital. Capitalism's operation at the cultural level makes it far more likely that people think *along capitalist lines*, even if unconsciously. Yet life in a consumer society involves an abundance of economic relations from which escape is near impossible. If you buy a Coca-Cola every day, you may not imagine that you have a relationship with the Coca-Cola Company itself, but you do. Even if you have never purchased a Coke in your life, you still arguably have some form of relationship with the Coca-Cola Company, because you *could* buy their product at any moment, you are exposed to their advertising, people around you may be buying and consuming their products, or working for them or their suppliers or wholesalers, they may be having an impact on your environment, and above all, there are people at that company sitting around thinking about how they can convince you to buy their product.

The Coca-Cola Company wants to be, and is, in your life whether or not you buy their products. As we will see below, so are Facebook and Twitter. You can't just opt out of the bits of capitalism you don't like. If the boardroom wants you, they will try everything they can think of to get you, and this is no different at Facebook Inc. than at more traditional corporations like tobacco giant Philip Morris International Inc.

When John Perry Barlow wrote his famous "A Declaration of the Independence of Cyberspace" in 1996, it was addressed to governments as if they were the sole holders of coercive power, to which consent to govern had not been given. Read alone, the line "Governments derive their just powers from the consent of the governed. You have neither solicited nor received ours" could be interpreted both easily and quite fittingly in today's world as if it were addressed to unwelcome corporate power on the internet, as opposed to governments, yet this would be a misreading of his intentions. As a whole, the document from which it comes is written as if corporate power had nothing to do with the internet and bore it no threat at all. Even in 1996 — the year after eBay was founded and two years after Amazon was founded — nothing could have been further from the truth. Barlow himself was punished for this naïvety when two hackers accessed his credit history from a company known as TRW and published it online, in order to show that the internet was subject to corporate power and not the utopia he claimed it to be. More than twenty years later, while virtually all governments extend their undemocratic or unethical policies online, the list of corporations that comprise existential threats to the internet in various ways is longer still. Barlow has since admitted that there was a wilfulness to his utopianism, saying in a 2015 interview that "the best way to invent the future is to predict it." Reading Barlow's "Declaration" as a textbook example of cyberutopianism, the complete lack of recognition of corporate influence it entails speaks volumes about the degree to which corporate influence has been able to maintain a low profile, and why it has been able to do so online.

It is no accident that our relationships are unwittingly entered into, or that the workings of capital are so much further out of sight. A central part of how modern capitalism deals with its potential customers, consumers, or clients, as well as with its workers, is in how it obscures the nature of its relations. Whether selling us social media or soda, exchanging with worker or customer, capitalism functions best when nobody questions the terms of the deal they are getting. Where the consumer is aware of being party to an exchange, the emphasis is always on what they will get, and how little they will have to give in return.

The most dangerous version of how our relationships with capital are obfuscated is when you don't realise you're participating in an exchange at all. Since we do not pay for most online services, we are distracted from the idea that they are businesses or that money is being made (or that this is being attempted). Because Facebook Inc. the company and Facebook the platform have the same name, people are even less likely to imagine that there is a second "Facebook" that they can't see, listed on the Nasdaq and trying to make as much money from them as possible, and the same goes for Twitter.

As journalist Chris Anderson has written, supposedly "free" products have long been a part of consumerism's long-term strategy to make money from us (2009), and nowhere is this more true than online. On parts of the internet away from social media, such as in news and media, users have come to expect something for nothing, and a number of websites that added paywalls have had to remove them again. Networks such as Facebook and Twitter have exploited this expectation and assumed a role in our lives such that we can trust that they are *there for us*. Indeed, the panic when they disappear or become unavailable is considerable: In 2014, the Los Angeles Police Department confirmed that people frequently call the police if they cannot access Facebook. But these networks are not *there for us*; they're there for themselves and for their shareholders. It's their platform, they make the rules, and when we use it, whatever we may feel we get from using social media, we do so entirely on their terms. If anything, we are there for them. Thus our relationship with social media corporations is often an exchange that appears not to be an exchange, and it is hard to make sure you are treated fairly in an exchange if you don't know you're participating in it. This is a dangerous situation that not only makes exploitation possible, but is designed to make it easy.

The most important aspect of understanding our relationships with the large enterprises, including those that design, host, and provide access to our digital lives, is to remember that companies like Visa, Nike, the Coca-Cola Company, McDonald's — or Facebook — act in relation to one key factor above any other: The pursuit of profit. No reader will need reminding that Facebook originates from a large US American corporation by the same name. Not a charity or an NGO, but a large, purely commercial organisation. Should we not ask how that corporation manages to pay its employees and shareholders, or how our use of the platform is connected with their need, like any company, to earn revenue in order to do so? What about Twitter? Who are the human beings who provide this service (or what seems to be a service) that has become so important my life? What do they get from this? Why is it free?

Social media platforms, and Facebook in particular, given its size, represent a new generation of enterprise that feeds off its relationships with users in far more sophisticated ways. Whereas the previous generation of enterprises focused on selling you a product and exploiting cheap labour and commodities from elsewhere in order to produce that product considerably more cheaply than they sold it for and pocketing the difference, social media enterprises are different. Instead of the consumption being the experience for which we pay, the consumption is free because it yields something *else* to the company that holds enormous value. As the increasingly common saying about digital services goes, "if it's free, you're the product." Companies such as Facebook, Twitter, and Google hold all the data you have uploaded in the course of your using their platforms, and in the terms you agree to as a condition of usage, you have given them pretty broad permission to do what they want with those data. The fact that 1.18 billion people (and growing) check Facebook at least once a day, for instance, means advertisers will spend a lot of money to access these people, and to target those users. According to its earnings reports, Facebook earned a net profit after tax of more than two billion dollars in the three months to June 30th 2016, 186% up on the same figure the year before. In the same period, Twitter grossed 535 million dollars from advertising. Beguiled by the illusion of receiving something for nothing, our usage therefore provides valuable data that generates billions of dollars per year in revenue, and which can be passed on to other companies who can use it to do things such as calculating our creditworthiness and offering us loans. This is what technology writer Shoshana Zuboff has called *surveillance capitalism* (2016).

Historically, each consumer-facing company has needed to find its own place in the emotional life of its customers and potential customers. Brand loyalty, word of mouth, and repeat purchases are all driven by this type of emotional relationship, and one of the primary means by which these relationships have been established has been advertising. Companies like Nike, Coca-Cola, and Apple have used expert marketing and branding, featuring slogans like "Just do it," "Life tastes good," and "Think different" to insert themselves into specific areas of consumers' lives so that they can become synonymous with particular wants, needs, and aspirations that will lead to sales.

Facebook in particular has made the fact that other businesses need this relationship with consumers into its core business: If Facebook cultivates a comprehensive, general relationship with the consumer and does the hard work of burrowing into their emotional lives, this proximity to the consumer makes them an essential service provider for other companies looking to generate sales. The more Facebook is a part of your life, the more effectively they can provide this service to their advertising clients.

While it may not be obvious to the vast majority of social media users, who are more likely just trying to get on and live their lives, that as a society we have come to develop such a dysfunctional and above all exploitative relationship with social media, we should not believe for a second that it is lost on the companies such as Facebook Inc. We've all been in bad relationships. The person possibly takes a lot from you, doesn't "have your back," treats you like you're expendable, doesn't care for you when you're sick, doesn't seem to appreciate you for who you are, or worst of all, just wants you for your money. In so far as each McDonald's customer, Apple iPhone owner, or Facebook user has their own separate relationship with those respective companies, the same is unfortunately true, and most of the time it is exactly this exploitative disposition that has allowed these companies to become so large.

Companies will always insist that they are motivated by loftier goals than plain profit or expansion. Google, for instance, long had the motto "Don't be evil," which is interesting not only because it acknowledges that the company is in a position to be "evil," should it choose to be, but because when Google restructured in October 2015, the motto was dropped entirely. Perhaps it was planning to be a bit more "evil"? In a more classic example, Facebook has insisted for years that its purpose is to "make the world more open and connected." As we will see below, this is a laughable euphemism given its actual business model, and should be seen as more akin to Coca-Cola's verbose mission statement "To refresh the world in mind, body and spirit. To inspire moments of optimism and happiness through our brands and actions," or L'Oréal's claim that you should spend money on their products "Because you're worth it" — in other words, it is a statement that has little if any relation to reality, and which is calculated to distract more gullible users or customers from the company's true objectives.

The only people who actually care about the intrinsic qualities of products themselves, beyond a means to extract profit, are consumers. The people who sell smartphones, sugared water, or unhealthy fried food don't need to believe in or enjoy their products in the same way they hope you will, and may not even consume or use their own products at all. Just as the executives who work at Coca-Cola are under no illusions that they exploit your thirst and desire for sugar to sell you Coke and Sprite at a considerable profit, when Facebook adds a new feature, they are not doing this because it's "cool." Whatever your subjective experience of using their platform, you are there for them to make money from, and the new feature is a way for them to extract that value from you more effectively. Your mental and physical health, and the health of the society in which you live, do not feature in the quarterly earnings conference call with the CFOs of such corporations.

Private lives, publicly listed

When a company floats on an exchange such as the Nasdaq, it reveals something about their prior aspirations and goals. It says that, in the end, they wanted to become part of a specific system of commodified corporate ownership and control, where profits are emphasised more than in any other. It buys into a belief that it doesn't matter what the company sells or how it makes its profits; as long as it manages to produce those profits the value of its shares increases. The very idea of holding shares in a corporation entails that, save possibly for voting on a few matters (if your shares allow), your position in relation to the company in which you own shares is purely about owning something that has value that can be sold on later, and which may provide you with a share of the profits in the meantime, by way of dividends. Publicly-listed companies with shareholders don't just have a relationship with their consumers, workers, users, and suppliers; these people all become secondary to appeasing shareholders, who expect regular dividend payments and that the value of their initial investment increases. Often, that means extracting as much value as possible from the company's other relationships — especially with consumers and workers — and from the environment, with little regard to the impact this may have.

The fact that most social networks have become large, publicly-listed corporations should therefore tell us something about their overall priorities. Romantic platitudes about how amazing social media are, or how they have "changed journalism" or "transformed social relationships," are even more eye-watering when you realise that the people running these platforms are only interested in these affordances to the extent that they may help the company make more money and push up its share price.

Writer Douglas Rushkoff recounts how, when Twitter floated as a publicly-listed company, he saw its co-founder Evan Williams on the front cover of the *Wall Street Journal* the morning of the IPO:

> Just under his chin they had printed the number $4.3 billion — the amount of money he made that day. […] Evan [who had also started Blogger and sold it to Google] had disrupted journalism with the blog and newsgathering with the tweet, but now he was surrendering all that disruption to the biggest, baddest industry of them all. When you're on the front page of the *Wall Street Journal*, receiving applause from all those guys in suits, it's not usually because you've done something revolutionary; it's because you have helped confirm financial capital's centrality to the whole scheme of human affairs.

Rushkoff is right to question whether the *use value* of Twitter or Blogger as a service, and the experiences and affordances they have provided, accord with the cold, hard, profit-driven orientation of a publicly-listed corporation controlled by "suits"; there is undoubtedly a mismatch. But this discordance is not because the founders have somehow "sold out," "surrendered" the "disruption," and joined in with the guys in the suits out of temptation. It is a discordance between the economic interests of the founders and the use of the platform for cultural and social purposes that are less focused on money, if at all.

The economic history of Silicon Valley, which can be traced all the way back to California's history as the site of a gold rush in the mid-nineteenth century, has always been about getting rich. When we see Steve Jobs say in a Nineties documentary that "When I was twenty-three I was worth a million dollars and when I was twenty-four I was worth ten million dollars and when I was twenty-five I was worth a hundred million dollars, but it was never about the money," we should be sceptical. Admittedly, there was a utopian, hippie element to Apple's vision for the role of computers, inspired by Stewart Brand's *Whole Earth Catalog*, but this was quickly displaced by business. If it wasn't about the money, why court rich investors and hire top-notch advertising consultants? The dot-com bubble, and the "web 2.0" businesses that followed it, among which Twitter is very much included, were no different, and represented a means for young, predominantly middle-class, US American millennials with a knowledge of coding to achieve levels of wealth previously unavailable without joining more traditional industries where there would have been considerable culture clash. The culture clash occurs instead at the moments Rushkoff describes: When founders achieve the extreme wealth to which they've aspired all along and these ambitions are revealed, despite communities having been enticed in the meantime to use digital platforms as part of their cultural and social lives. The culture clash is between the founders and the users; between the shareholders and the users. It is the users who are betrayed at these moments. The lesson here is that you cannot bring any aspect of your life onto these platforms without becoming part of somebody's get-rich plan; somebody's quarterly revenues; somebody's dividend payment. If you want to use Facebook, use it, but remember that that is what you are participating in. However quiet the operations and realisations of these large-scale economic ambitions might be, they are always there. There is no "pure" social media.

Changes to terms and conditions

One good example of how the hidden power dynamic in our relationships with social media corporations can manifest itself is in the sudden changes to terms and conditions that arise when these corporations alter the direction of their business, especially after stock-market flotations and acquisitions. Photo- and video-sharing platform Instagram, acquired by Facebook in April 2012 for one billion dollars, tried in December of that same year to roll out a change to its terms and conditions that would make it more compatible with advertising. The most contentious addition to its terms read:

> To help us deliver interesting paid or sponsored content or promotions, you agree that a business or other entity may pay us to display your username, likeness, photos (along with any associated metadata), and/or actions you take, in connection with paid or sponsored content or promotions, without any compensation to you.

This passage, although ultimately not included in Instagram's terms and conditions after a major public backlash, is typical of the broader pattern of social media corporations: You give us something, and we sell it for advertising purposes. Similarly, in January 2012 when Google revised the terms of use for all its products, it was in order to track users across all their devices and all products. In August 2016, Facebook-owned messaging app WhatsApp, trusted by users because of its end-to-end encryption, announced a change to its terms of use that allowed it to pass your phone number and user-profile data to its parent company Facebook, despite having promised never to do so, although a subtly placed opt-out switch was available.

The lawyers who write these terms and the executives who sanction them know very well not only that you are unlikely to read them, but that the products they govern are used habitually; indeed they could scarcely be ignorant of the research that shows these patterns, outlined in Chapter Two of this book. It is an equivalent situation to coffee, tobacco, sugar, or alcohol companies suddenly changing their "terms and conditions"; the consumption would continue because the product in question is one on which the user depends. When designer and speaker Aral Balkan says of the tech community that "There are only two professions that call the people who use their products 'users.' One is drug dealers, the other is us," this is a helpful reminder of the context in which these changes take place. A sudden (as far as users are concerned) change to terms and conditions is the most efficient way to bring users onto a new legal footing. There is some kind of news headline almost every time these changes occur, and the column inches at the *Guardian* are predictably uniform. Save for some major outcry as experienced by Instagram in 2012 however, most such changes are final and relatively swift. The small minority of users who decide they are unhappy enough with the change to stop using the service are invariably pulled back in again by the need to "fill the void" with social interaction and other distractions such as pictures of food and kittens.

Are we not human?

The fact that social media corporations' very existence, not to mention quarterly profits, are dependent on our continuing usage might make it seem as though it is users who theoretically can decide the fate of such companies. However, the compulsive behaviours and psychological functions of social media make it very difficult for a lot of people to leave; very difficult not to be exploited, in other words. Designer and campaigner Aral Balkan has argued passionately that our relationship with these companies is such that we are being "farmed" without our knowledge. There is certainly something to this. Our humanity, our social relations, our cultures, have undoubtedly become a highly valuable, commodified form of data which we give away unwittingly. When Facebook upgraded its straightforward "Like" button to include five other gestures ("Love," "Haha," "Wow," "Sad," and "Angry") this only meant a richer harvest — more data and more accurate data — but users loved this change for the most part. People even made cookies that looked like the new buttons, to celebrate. What more fitting tribute to the ways that your emotional reactions to affective stimuli like pictures of cookies are harvested for commercial gain but the consumption of real cookies that look like the means by which this data capture takes place!? You honestly couldn't make it up.

In so far as the data and insights collected about us are sold, we are being sold, Balkan argues, and the only other time human beings have ever been sold in the past was called *slavery*, he has said, somewhat provocatively. "It's about time to ask ourselves, however, what are we to call the business of selling everything about a person that makes them who they are *apart* from their body?" he asks. I find myself wondering what Frederick Douglass or Harriet Tubman would have made of that comparison, which I leave as an open question, but the point he makes is an important one. As slightly controversial metaphors go, Balkan has more. The way digital life is being slowly subsumed into specific businesses that exploit us for data, and particularly the way this strategy is visited on people around the world who have as-yet experienced no other internet — known in Silicon Valley as "the next five billion" — is akin to colonialism, he argues. Again, I flinch and wonder whether psychologist and anti-colonialist revolutionary philosopher Frantz Fanon would have agreed, but initiatives such as Facebook's *Free Basics* program in India — part of its *Internet.org* initiative which seeks to provide a very limited form of access to Facebook and a carefully chosen array of news outlets instead of full internet access — are extremely problematic, as is their patronising contempt for the as-yet unconnected people they claim to serve. Perhaps this is one reason why, at the time of writing, *Free Basics* has been indefinitely halted by an Indian court.

While slavery and colonialism are probably not the most sensitive of comparators to the digital exploitation undertaken by companies like Facebook Inc. on their users, it's worth considering — while we're discussing heroic members of the struggle against human oppression such as Fanon, Douglass, and Tubman — that what they would all have agreed on, and all subverted in their own lives in different ways, was the dehumanisation that has so often formed the foundation on which brutality, exploitation, and other forms of injustice are effected. To Facebook, Twitter, Google, and any other company that derives its business from the data we generate using its products, the full breadth of our humanity is only interesting in so far as it generates more accurate, more detailed, and thus more valuable data. Whether we are reduced to animals, to colonial subjects, to three fifths of a person, to labour costs, to commodities, or, by extension, to data, dehumanisation is dehumanisation. There is in the business models of social media corporations, however you twist it and however much their PR and marketing departments might claim otherwise, the unmistakeable stench of dehumanisation as the data collected from users becomes a commodity and thus a form of capital. Simply put, such businesses do not accord with the respect that all humanity should be afforded. This, I suspect, is what Aral Balkan means.

*　*　*

If nothing else, the pseudo-legal copy-and-paste status updates people occasionally post in the vain hope of preventing the appropriation of the materials they upload to Facebook show that users know that social media platforms are owned by companies that may not always act in accordance with their own interests. So why don't we wake up? When it comes to the companies that enable or mediate our digital lives, we do know after all that Facebook isn't just some free app or a website provided to us out of goodwill, and neither are Twitter or WhatsApp or Instagram or Weibo or VKontakte.

It is tempting to believe that if people *really* knew how much Facebook, Twitter, Google, Snapchat, and other companies were exploiting them, they would be so indignant and outraged that they would find a way to forego the practical benefits of services like Gmail or the emotion-regulation patterns outlined in Chapter Two (or seek them elsewhere) and close their accounts. But as any regular Facebook or Gmail user will attest, this is a vain hope at best. All companies who operate on this business model know that this is their Achilles heel; they know that just as users are free to begin using their software at any time, users are also theoretically free to cease doing so, and the exploitation would end — so why don't they?

Part of the answer, as I have said above, is how we are taught by capitalism to think according to its logic. Everything about capitalism encourages us to participate, and to *enjoy*, hence the hedonic use of social media. To abstain is to resist this powerful temptation on seemingly political grounds alone. Another answer, however, is in how corporations such as Google and Facebook worm their way into our lives. The common consensus is that they need to find out what is meaningful and important to us so that these data can be sold to advertisers, but they have at least one more purpose: The companies behind social networks know that our primary relationship with their platforms is emotional. The more they can mediate and become synonymous with meaningful and emotionally important areas of your life, the less likely you are to leave them or make their data collection from you more difficult, and the more likely you are to forgive their unilateral changes to terms and conditions, unexpected removal of favoured features, or forced implementation of unfavourable ones, and create social pressures on your friends to sign up, participate, and stay.

Often, the same criticisms are levelled at social media corporations, and especially Facebook, as at Google in respect of the data-driven business model, but there are important differences. Aral Balkan's stinging criticisms of Google's various devious strategies to encircle our lives with free but invaluable products such as Gmail are justly deserved, and applicable to Facebook to an extent, but while Google might have claimed your email, web searches, documents and calendars, social media come much further into your life and into far more intimate and meaningful areas of it, and this is a very important difference. Whatever we may say of the manipulative and exploitative practices of Google, most people will still find easy justification for the use of their products on practical grounds: effective web search is useful, email is useful, calendars are useful, and Microsoft Office-compatible documents that can be simultaneously edited in real-time by many authors in different locations with nothing but a web browser are *really* useful. Knowing how exploitative they are, it pains me to admit it, but admitting their usefulness should not undermine the ethical criticisms of Google at all; rather, it can be a part of them. Google knew that these would be the most useful services for us, so they implemented these services as favourably as possible, or purchased them in some cases, so that we would all flock to them, forsaking other less practical options, as well as their competitors Microsoft, Apple, and Yahoo. That doesn't mean the products are bad, it means the underlying exploitative strategy is bad.

After more than ten years it is clear that "social media," and Facebook especially, have culminated in a refinement and advancement of the basic data-harvesting strategies pioneered by Google. They are the next generation of the same idea. The twist that social media have introduced into this pattern is that whereas we at least know the ways we are dependent on Google because we know what their products are *for*, Facebook and Twitter make their specific role in your life far more malleable. All Twitter does is limit you to 140 characters; it has no other purpose besides that which its users give it. Even Twitter's 140-character limit, however, is existentially well-defined compared to Facebook. What is Facebook actually for? Ask a thousand different people and you'll get a thousand different answers.

Whereas the "revolution" in web 2.0 was supposedly that the content would now come from users as opposed to publishers or site owners, a further evolution of this paradigm has quietly taken place in the sense that now the very purpose of the platform comes from the users too. Platform developers simply sit back and watch what users do with the software they have created, then build in new features to support that activity. On Twitter, "@" mentions, hashtags, retweets, and direct messages were not part of the original platform; users began to employ the @ symbol to address one another, for example, and eventually the feature was built into the core functionality of the platform. Some people use Twitter for subject-specific news, some for shameless self-promotion, some to build up new business, and some for entertainment, and the platform does not discriminate between these different uses. Facebook is used for so many purposes related to so many different areas of our lives that even identifying them all would be a significant challenge. This *telic vagueness* is arguably a further manifestation of how the nature of your relationship with the social media corporations collecting data from you is obscured. If the very purpose of a social network appears to come from you, the user, and from the things that are meaningful in your life, then your subjective experience of using that platform is going to feel far more natural and give you the feeling of a lot more agency.

With pre-digital technologies of modernity, even if they were mass-produced, it was much easier from the eventual consumer's perspective to identify *why* the technology was originally invented, what exactly it allowed us to do that we could not do before, which areas of life it applied to, and crucially, whether or not we actually needed it. The electric toaster, as a simple example, had a nice clear purpose; it was invented to make the singeing of slices of bread more convenient. If you don't like bread, you probably don't own a toaster. Sure enough, that is how our adoption of the web started, in the 1990s. Using the web was once a domain-specific activity, which some people called "surfing the web." An early ad for the Apple iMac, presented by actor Jeff Goldblum, even compared the iMac to a toaster in how simple it made internet access.

Today however, whether applying for a visa or booking a table at a restaurant, plagiarising a blogpost for a college essay, or checking to see whether one of your students has plagiarised a suspiciously cogent passage that appears to be in a different font, the web as a whole has become sufficiently important in enough domains of life that it no longer has a clear or obvious purpose. This in itself is a fairly harmless development, as long as people without internet access are not excluded from important public functions, such as paying their taxes, that may be increasingly carried out online. Perhaps this general role that the web has developed is why, for a while, it was impossible to go to a media-related conference without somebody comparing the invention of the web to that of the printing press by Johannes Gutenberg in 1440 — it's a technology that is used for nearly everything.

The web being so large and full of noise, however, means that a demand has arisen to filter and organise our use of it — particularly as the great increase in connection speeds has enabled more and more entertainment to take place there. Enter social media. Whereas the web of the Nineties usually involved entering a domain name into the address bar on your web browser, most web journeys now begin with either a Google search or a social media timeline. Social media are increasingly becoming our gateway to the overall web. Indeed, according to BuzzFeed's industry insights, social networks have overtaken search as the largest driver of traffic, accounting for 32% of all web traffic on average, and Facebook alone now drives 25%. To help that sink in, I will write it again — an average of 25% of web traffic to other websites comes via Facebook alone (Wong, 2015). As part of this process, the cheerful "worldwide web" of amateur hand-built HTML pages, with their garish colours and animated gifs, has been superseded by a web experience in which our agency has been reduced to the choice of whether to click or not; keep scrolling or not;

"like," comment, both, or neither. Every year that I teach my students HTML it feels more and more alien, yet it is the fabric of every web page, and many smartphone apps. So alienated have we become from Tim Berners-Lee's original vision of how this medium should be used that it feels as though I were teaching them Ancient Greek. The ever-expanding role of social media also increasingly limits our choices about whether to stay on social media platforms or not. As the web has grown in its scope, social networks have positioned themselves as the shiny, easy-to-use gateways to the generalised web — whatever you want or need from it — but especially when you feel empty. Once your music provider, say Spotify, is using your Facebook account to authenticate you, you cannot leave Facebook, even temporarily, without losing access to your music subscription. "Sign in with Facebook" is not, perhaps, the convenience it might appear to be. Facebook don't provide a free authentication service for other websites out of the goodness of their hearts — it's a trap to make as much as possible of the rest of the web, and of our lives, conditional on having a Facebook account. This generality and *telic vagueness* has allowed them to weave themselves into the fabric of our everyday lives in a way that technologies such as toasters, cars, ball-point pens, and newspapers never have, and this means we can never leave.

Mediatedness and virtuality

In a speech at the University of Cambridge on the relationship of Facebook to the journalism industry, Emily Bell remarked that social media "hasn't just swallowed journalism, it has swallowed everything. It has swallowed political campaigns, banking systems, personal histories, the leisure industry, retail, even government and security." While at first glance this might have sounded deterministic, a more likely reading is that she was ascribing a very specific strategy and business style to the people that run social-networking sites, and especially Facebook. As strategies go, placing yourself between the customer and everything in their lives that is meaningful to them is pretty clever, if brazen.

They say happiness is in the little things. Think for a moment — what are the most important things in your day-to-day life beyond survival? Your social structures? Your interests? Your family? Events such as birthdays, holidays, and anniversaries? How you entertain yourself and keep yourself informed is pretty important, as is keeping a finger on the pulse of what people around you are enjoying. These are exactly the things without which you feel alienated and empty, as we have seen in Chapter Three. Orson Welles once famously said that "We're born alone, we live alone, we die alone. Only through our love and friendship can we create the illusion for the moment that we're not alone," and somewhere at Facebook, somebody has surely noted this down. Social networks pay attention to which aspects of people's lives will make them feel happy, and try to become synonymous with these areas of life.

Facebook is the champion practitioner of this strategy. Birthdays are a good example. They can't just be birthdays anymore — they have to be mediated and orchestrated by Facebook. "Marcus, we hope that you had a great birthday! Want to thank your friends for their birthday wishes?" they ask me, the day after mine. As a matter of fact, a small number of thoughtful friends had taken the time to send me some sort of birthday greeting via Facebook, and I was planning to thank them all for these genuine and much-appreciated gestures, but I was surprised to see Facebook actively suggesting I do this. Facebook birthday greetings are nothing new, but involving themselves in my birthday even the day after? I might have wondered, were I not in the middle of writing this book: What's in it for them?

With social media, you never have to go too far to find an answer to that question. All the same, this simple array of birthday-related features provides a useful opportunity to explore the strategy deployed by Facebook to use information about what will be salient and important to you, in a way that is subjectively pleasurable at best, unnoticeable at worst, to embed its place in the daily lives of its users and legitimise itself as a generalised lifestyle technology.

Obviously the ritual of a birthday is something that will vary widely with social inequality, culture, and geography, but rich or poor, they are generally a meaningful and important celebration of a person's having *survived* and grown for an exact number of years, almost defiant in the face of inevitable ageing and mortality. Facebook knows when its users' birthdays are because users are forced to provide this information when they create their accounts in order to "prove" their age. Many people enjoy Facebook knowing this information because when it's their birthday, Facebook's user interface encourages other users to write a greeting on that person's profile page, or "timeline." Facebook is far from alone among technology companies using your date of birth in this way: LinkedIn, Twitter, and Skype also have birthday-greeting functionalities built in.

A genuine birthday greeting from one friend to another is a longstanding tradition in many cultures; a matter of interpersonal communication between two friends, family members, or some other social relationship. To communicate this sentiment can scarcely be anything other than kind and caring, and we are afforded a range of communication options and technologies for the purpose, from a hand-written card delivered by post, to the most cursory digital "HBD xx" on a Facebook wall. To do so, in concert with other people, on Facebook, however, should not merely be regarded as just one more way to express that you are thinking of somebody on their birthday.

Birthdays are big business, too — even for kids. In the UK, parents spent over two billion pounds (2.5 billion dollars) per year on children's birthday parties. There is very little research quantifying the amount that adults spend specifically on marking each other's or their own birthdays, but capitalism has for a long time been able to turn your "special day" to its advantage. Even the song "Happy Birthday" was long claimed as the exclusive intellectual property of

Warner/Chappell Inc. — requiring an expensive royalty fee — until a 2015 lawsuit finally had this preposterous claim declared invalid.

Rather than there being any intrinsic significance to the day you were born, birthdays turn out just to be an example of a meaningful event in time, and are one of many domains in which this knowledge about you is used in ways that are intended to be meaningful and to vary the — Facebook assumes — otherwise uniform course of your daily life. The appropriation of such events for business purposes is an old trick. If you want to sell to people, you have to know what will be resonant to them, and it is events that introduce some semblance of variation and meaning over the monotony of everyday life that will often be most potent. This is surely one reason why, in 2012, Facebook reimagined the user profile page as a "timeline" with a strict chronological focus. New Year's Eve, Christmas, Valentine's Day, Halloween, Mother's Day and Father's Day, weddings, graduations, christenings, and even funerals are all arguably part of how, in a temporal context, mainstream culture tacitly converts the emotional importance of our significant others, parents, families, and friends into a reason to buy certain products, trust their products, or behave in other commercially helpful ways. Halloween — a completely secular, made up ritual — is a good example. According to research carried out for HBO's *Last Week Tonight with John Oliver*, Americans spend 2.2 billion dollars on candy every Halloween — nearly half the total amount they spend every year. In other areas, it is becoming more commonplace to criticise the ways in which capitalism uses such days to get into our lives. Valentine's Day, as another example, now meets with a healthy degree of annual resistance. Under the model of capitalist realism described by Mark Fisher, however, even this resistance may be in danger of becoming part of the overall capitalist ritual. *Time Out* magazine, for instance, often makes recommendations for things for singles to do on Valentine's Day. But why do (read: buy or consume) anything?

Like any business, Facebook's understanding of what is meaningful for its users is essential. While mainstream capitalism has difficulty going beyond standard themes of achievement, birth, marriage, love, Facebook is a self-customising software platform that is configured both by its users and by its developers to provide a distinct experience to each user. Media and metadata are easily generated based on the information Facebook already has, such as who knows who, and roughly when they became "friends." It is in this capacity that much of its power lies to mediate — and become — almost any area of our lives that it thinks will be meaningful.

One morning in London in June 2016, as rain lashes down outside, Facebook greets me with: "It's the first day of summer, Marcus! Hello sun, it's been a while." Despite the fact that many other users will also have seen an identical message, this is followed by a "share" button. The same techniques are used to cling onto whichever other areas of your life are likely to be most resonant, including your politics, your memories with friends about things that happened in the past, and your solidarity with people in (select) other parts of the world where higher-profile disasters and acts of terrorism have occurred. Below are a few examples of these:

In December 2014, Facebook caused a backlash by introducing a feature called "Year in Review" that showed users a summarised account of the calendar year that was drawing to a close. The feature had assumed that your year had been, on balance, a positive one, and invited users to reflect on their year from this perspective. "It's been a great year! Thanks for being a part of it," the cheery notice said. "Eric, here's what your year looked like!" it told one blogger, Eric Meyer, whose young daughter had died that year, bearing a picture of her face surrounded by figures dancing and balloons. "Yes, my year looked like that. True enough. My year looked like the now-absent face of my little girl. It was still unkind to remind me so forcefully," he wrote (Meyer, 2014). One comment below the article in which this was relayed offered: "This year I went through divorce. A few months after my separation, Facebook suggested via a push message to my phone that I befriend my ex-wife's lover." Users may have forgotten what they posted years ago, but Facebook remembers. Reminders of your earlier Facebook posts, and the phases of life that they are said to represent, are also offered on a near-constant basis. A feature known as "On This Day" looks back at your prior activity, going back over a decade in the case of some users, to see what else occurred on the same date, and on finding something, asks you if you would like to share your (read: Facebook's) memory of that day, which seems like a recipe for further "algorithmic cruelty."

In August 2015, Facebook marked the 95th anniversary of women's suffrage in the United States in a similarly overoptimistic fashion, posting an image at the top of users' home screens that, in the words of a report on news website Daily Dot, "included women of many racial and ethnic backgrounds posing in homage to the iconic image of Rosie the Riveter, to the backdrop of a patriotic 'We Voted!' button." Besides the hokey opportunism, there was just one other pretty major problem: "August 26, 1920 was the day that *white* women achieved the right to vote in America. For women of color — many of whom were silenced, ignored or racially discriminated against within the early feminist movement — white supremacy still reigned supreme at many ballot boxes; their right to vote was far from achieved." Facebook also marks International Women's Day every year with a similar-looking graphic, although so far without outcry.

In November 2015, when armed gunmen killed 130 people in Paris, Facebook's official page on its own platform posted a version of the Facebook logo, superimposed with a French flag and accompanied with the message "We stand together. *#JeSuisParis*" and introduced a tool whereby users could superimpose a French flag over their own profile photo "to support France and the people of Paris." They also separately implemented a means for people in the Paris region to notify the friends and family to whom they were connected on Facebook that they were safe, a feature which had also been used in other disasters such as the Pakistan-Afghanistan earthquake two weeks prior to the events in Paris. Controversy ensued once again because the same features were not also made available in response to a separate terrorist attack in Lebanon that had occurred only a day prior to those in Paris.

For the UK's referendum on leaving the European Union and for major elections in a number of Western countries, Facebook has implemented a specialised feature that allows you to share that you have voted. The same question can be asked about all of these cases: Does Facebook really care that you exercise your democratic duty, or does it care that you express that you have indeed done so via Facebook?

The technique is not only applied to Facebook as a product or software interface, but also as a company. In July 2016, against the backdrop of increasing public outrage about US police officers murdering innocent African Americans, Facebook reportedly displayed a large "Black Lives Matter" graphic on an outdoor screen on its campus in reference to the campaign started in August 2014 of the same name. Admittedly, compared to solidarity with victims of an awful terrorist attack, or even with the LGBT community who had finally been granted the right to marry the people they love, backing Black Lives Matter is a far more politically risky move on Facebook's part, but we already know that affect and arousal are what Facebook deals in. If you're happy to keep using Facebook without reading the terms and conditions, whether you love or hate their support for Black Lives Matter or gay marriage won't put you off using Facebook either. The idea that the company would innocently decide, for ideological reasons alone, that it must support the Black Lives Matter campaign, is an extremely naïve one.

Perhaps the high-ups at Facebook may sometimes desire that the company takes a stand on global issues that they deem to be important in themselves, but even if consciously that were all there was to it, this would not change the fact that however well-intentioned and wholesome these interventions, these same issues become — from a subjective user's perspective — conflated with Facebook both as a functional tool and as a brand. Not only can Facebook be taking a stand while simultaneously mediating inescapably emotional issues for its users in ways that are commercially useful, without the need for mutual exclusivity, the two processes can become entangled to the point that they operate indistinguishably. Whether or not Facebook's executives care about Black Lives Matter, the company and the platform will inevitably benefit from being the means by which their users engage with that debate.

Other social media apps and networks incorporate mediation in comparable, if more subtle, ways. LinkedIn bizarrely allows you to observe the "anniversary" of your connections having worked in their current job, as if anybody actually celebrates this. Rather, it is simply an example of the same strategy in play, and employment dates are simply the data you have given LinkedIn. At the other end of the scale, but according to the same strategy, Snapchat varies the filters you are able to apply to your own face depending on location, as well as time. If you happen to visit Disneyland, for example, Disney-specific filters become available. Twitter tends to use a more subtle approach, sticking to time-specific occurrences such as major elections, and sporting events such as the World Cup or the Olympics, embellishing the appearance of hashtags that are in heavy use in connection with these events and providing limited, short-term functionalities such as means to keep scores. If you wanted to pick three more capitalism-friendly bodies than Disney, Fifa, and the International Olympic Committee, you would be hard pressed to find them.

Subtlety is just as well, because Facebook's more explicit efforts often smack of pure desperation. The day after the Rio 2016 Olympics, Facebook gushes: "Thank you, Olympians! Over the past two weeks we've witnessed the world's greatest athletes compete in Rio. With full hearts and great pride we congratulate them on their achievements." Whatever you think of this statement or of the Olympic Games in general, we should be highly sceptical that anybody at Facebook has added this message to the platform because of a genuine intention that Olympic athletes be sufficiently congratulated. In order to be as general as possible in your life, Facebook needs to claim the Olympics too. In fact, Facebook and the Olympic Games serve each other's interests very well. The Olympics provide the perfect, affectively stimulating fodder for the social media timeline, distracting people from the emotional distress in their own lives. In doing so they are simultaneously able to fulfil what has come to be their de-facto primary role, which is to draw the attention of the masses away from the bigger picture of what else is happening in the world.

As noted in the first chapter, the fact that "social media" have become known by that signifier should be seen not so much as a reflection of what they offer their users, so much as what their users give them. Social media have become increasingly generalised because they have deliberately harnessed our basic human sociality to become so. By characterising themselves as "social," they can go everywhere your friends go. The development of Facebook Messenger, when the world was already full of instant-messaging platforms, is the result of precisely this strategy. If you tell your friends about something, Facebook wants you to feel that their platform is the natural choice, so that you will have to tell them, too. Writing in 2008, when Facebook had just fifty-nine million users, author Tom Hodgkinson wrote of Facebook that "we are seeing the commodification of human relationships, the extraction of capitalistic value from friendships." This is true, but commodification is old-hat entry-level capitalism compared to how social media work. What social media, and especially Facebook, do is effectively *parasitise* various aspects of their users in order to become part of their lives: Their sense of technology as something that should work for them, their boredom, their depression, their existential angst, their desire to be appreciated, and their existing social relationships. And sociality isn't just about friends. LinkedIn has worked tirelessly to do the same with your professional connections and aspirations, and Twitter has positioned itself even more generally still: Some people, such as journalists, use it more for work and information, and others for sociality or hedonic media consumption, making it both a mediator between you and sources of information and entertainment and, thanks to follower counts, a numerical measurer of seeming authority and importance. Whether for work or personal social interaction, however, sociality isn't just about you. Your "friends" have "friends," who have "friends," who have "friends," and so on, until most of the people around you have accounts, even if they don't use them. Consequently, while adoption of these platforms (or access to the internet at all) is not even across the world, entire societies have been absorbed by and willingly reproduced their social relations on Facebook, Twitter, and so forth in places where these platforms have a greater degree of penetration. Because the platforms are intimately tied to meaningful interpersonal relationships, their use becomes almost as obvious and natural as those relationships themselves. This appropriation and absorption of the people in your life who are already meaningful and important is one key means by which social media get their power.

Mark Zuckerberg must have been delighted when, three years after Facebook was launched, the launch of the iPhone made it possible to take Facebook to bed with you. Two billion people now own smartphones, and a 2016 study reported that one in ten people even admit to having checked their smartphone *during sex*. But why would Mark Zuckerberg (and everybody else at Facebook) have been so happy that you could take Facebook to bed with you? Just as a train can only go where there are tracks, lifestyle software, and the forms of capitalism dependent on it, requires lifestyle *hardware* in order that they have the means to become a physically integrated part of your life, and the generality of social media is something that has been enabled and extended by smartphones and generalised hardware. Perhaps this explains why Facebook has been investing so heavily in virtual-reality hardware outfit Oculus VR, which it bought in 2014.

Ultimately the smartphone handset is a vestigial design based on the century-old idea of a telephone, but when it comes to the mediation of daily life itself, wearable technology, virtual reality, and other forms of pervasive hardware are far more valuable long-term prospects, which is exactly why everyone in Silicon Valley is talking about them. A new technology known as *teledildonics* even allows virtual sexual stimulation to be applied to the genitals, using a complex system of sensors and pads.

The process of constant adaptation

The process by which social media's increasingly general presence in modern life has arisen should not be overlooked. Digital technology is not static; its features are not fixed, and it is in the nature of how software is written and then executed by a chip that their changes may be imperceptible to the user from one day to the next. Software engineers are excellent at making use of their own fortuitous mistakes and unexpected user reactions. Indeed, this is necessary. Any software programmer knows that users do not take lightly to being coerced; it is much better to use user behaviours and reactions to guide software development than the reverse, and nowhere is this truer than in mass-market, everyday web-based software like webmail and social networks. "@" mentions, "retweets," and "hashtags" on Twitter were all the ideas of its users, and subsequently incorporated into the basic working of the platform. This process is not always so unilateral, however. While the development of social media over the last decade or so might seem like a very large-scale version of this gently adaptive process, we would be foolish to be so naïve. Just like evolution in the natural world, accidental changes rarely survive into the future unless they are beneficial, but beneficial to whom?

If the users owned and were creating their own software, such as in the case of Firefox, GNU/Linux or WordPress, the answer to this question would be: The users! But we should remember that programmers employed by a large corporation, like any other employee, will always be instructed and managed with a second imperative in mind: Profit. Even if it is not entirely clear yet how they can profit from making a given change to their platform, they will do it anyway if they think that it will build a foundation on which it will be easier to generate additional profits in the future. Even if sharing your weight loss on Facebook or checking your Twitter mentions while driving is somehow useful to you, usefulness to end-users themselves comes second to benefits for the owners of the technology, or its shareholders, when the technology in question is proprietary. Facebook's pledge to "make the world more open and connected," for example, may be enough of a vapid marketing euphemism that we can smell it a mile away, but inside the meeting rooms and corridors of Facebook's various campuses, it is inconceivable that they could not have realised a long time ago exactly how general their platform would become, and what kind of role it could come to play in people's lives, if they played their cards right. Full-steam ahead, they decided.

Facebook, for example, may occasionally have angered its users by adding or removing some feature or other, but the number of changes that have taken place between the Facebook of 2005 (when this author first joined it) and the Facebook of 2017 are thousands and thousands more, most of which were barely noticed. While most consumer culture, particularly in a postmodern society, aims to present itself as perennially new, consumer software genuinely is subject to near constant change. Social media were so termed because they are an extension of our media, and of how we are informed and entertained, but this is changing faster than ever. While this may often be a bid not to be left behind, the ongoing change provides an opportunity for other types of adaptation.

Lisa Gitelman and Geoffrey Pingree (2003) argue that most media pass through a phase of novelty that is characterised by an identity crisis, before settling down:

when new media emerge in a society, their place is at first ill defined, and their ultimate meanings or functions are shaped over time by that society's existing habits of media use (which, of course, derive from experience with other, established media), by shared desires for new uses, and by the slow process of adaptation between the two. The "crisis" of a new medium will be resolved when the perceptions of the medium, as well as its practical uses, are somehow adapted to existing categories of public understanding about what that medium does for whom and why.

The adoption of pre-digital technologies is usually a story with a beginning, middle, and in some cases an end, but while this same narrative is ascribed to the adoption of the web, and subsequently of social media, their story is different. Instead, it is a case of constant cyclical adaptation and re-adaptation: We adapt to the technology and it is then adapted to us by its creators. Of course, capitalism has entailed a pressure to "innovate" for as long as it has existed, provided that there are competitive reasons for doing so, but as any software engineer will know, this has become an imperative with digital products and services: Just look at the number of "available updates" offered by the App Store on an Apple laptop or iPhone, or the fact that iTunes always seems to have a new version available for download. Another glimpse at this imperative is afforded when we consider the plight of bygone social networks such as MySpace that failed to "innovate." At the time of writing, there is even concern that Twitter is facing the same fate. While it might be terribly cliché to assert that "the only constant is change," this is an intrinsic quality of intangible products such as software. All that is coded melts into thin air if it is not regularly tinkered with, updated, and expanded. While the web is old enough to have a history, at its leading edge, it is *always new*.

Crucially, this means the questions we ask about its role in our lives need to be constantly re-asked, and our critique adapted accordingly such that we maintain a clear view. Over enough time, the constant modification of any software-based technology can cause it to evolve so much that it undergoes a complete change in kind, and that is what has happened with the web, and especially with those platforms who have managed to stay relevant over that period of time: Facebook, Twitter, and Google. While this change in kind may well be part of the thinking of those who have effected it, it is not always perceptible to those who use the technology subject to the change. The makers of the software can completely change their motivations and strategy whilst having near complete control over how, and indeed whether, this change is reflected in the underlying product. This imbalance results in a power inequality and divergence of intention that is inevitably unethical.

Mining new areas of value

Hopefully it should now be clear that as we "fill the void" we are participating in the enrichment of social media corporations and the companies that pay them for advertising, filling the pockets of Wall Street and Silicon Valley. In Marxian terms, social media are both superstructure *and* base. There is something harsh about this scenario. Our use of social media platforms may well be injudicious, but it is compulsive and emotionally driven, born of a variety of forms of misery, while the proprietors of social networking sites are far more rational and calculating. Capitalism is invariably desperate to find new areas of surplus value, even if it means exploitation of the very emotional distress that it has itself created. In deriving value from our poor emotions themselves, and from our desire to block these out, social media represent a development of capitalism's exploitative, dehumanising tendencies. Social media have quietly metamorphosed into what is probably the ultimate capitalist technology, in two distinct senses. Firstly, their generality makes them very growth-friendly: Why provide for (or sell to) users in just one area of life when you can provide in all areas, with increasing levels of personal intimacy? Secondly, they comprise a means of cheaply distributing software that continually extracts an extremely valuable commodity from us in vast quantities. Ultimately, since capitalism produces both technology and unhappiness, it should be no surprise when capitalism produces technologies that exploit our unhappiness. But what does this mean for the culture and media shared on social networks, and how should we respond? These questions are dealt with in the next and final chapter.

— FIVE —

Identifying the politics of content

Two consequences of filling the void

When we look at the picture created by Chapters One to Four of this book, we see that it is a worrying one overall. At this point, it may be helpful to summarise the arguments presented so far, in order to see this picture clearly.

Despite the fact that social media affect us in a variety of ways that are not good for us, we can't seem to resist using them. The story of the web's arrival into our lives is one that has generally encouraged a positivistic, nouveau-enlightenment, practically-oriented view of, at best, what new capabilities it provides us, and at worst, what the new technologies *make* us do. But the failure of control some of us exhibit in relation to social media reveals a different relationship with these technologies entirely, one that is often habitual and compulsive. The word "addiction" is even thrown around.

The emphasis of the debate about social media has largely been about identity and the self, what we post in that context, and why, but this picture shows us that in the end this may have been an incomplete analysis. It is a common misconception to understand technology as something that acts on and shapes us, but it is important that we instead see both social networks themselves and our use of them as being produced *by* culture. More specifically, and regardless of where they are actually used, social networks are the product of first-world late-capitalist culture, which is increasingly pervaded by an economic logic. Examining the nature of our strangely compulsive relationship with social media has therefore required that this culture be unpicked. In doing so, two interlocking aspects of this culture are revealed as being particularly important:

Firstly, it is a culture that promotes *consumption*. Nearly everything is a consumable commodity, including media and culture themselves, which have become commodified into "content." Social networks, in fact, must be understood above all as a reconfiguration of the web into a form that makes commodified media consumption as easy and as appealing as possible. But it is not enough to say that we are simply consuming media which have been commodified; this consumption is driven by some very interesting and specific processes that connect with the experience of life in a consumer society in general. Whether the content of the media is kittens, pictures of food, or highly subjective, opinion-based articles, the common thread in most timeline-based social media is that they provide an emotionally arousing experience that helps us to momentarily feel happy, sad, angry, proud, nostalgic, curious, etc. The specific nature or content of the media they encounter is only important to users of timeline media in so far as they are consuming a subjective emotional experience that provides much-needed distraction from the emotional reality in which they would otherwise find themselves, by way of a blast of affective stimulation.

Secondly, "first-world" late-capitalist culture places considerable stress on its participants. The idea that the so-called "first world" is happy while the "third world" suffers and struggles to survive, mocked with the idea of "first-world problems," is also superficial and highly simplistic. Different forms of suffering are produced in the developed and developing worlds, and for different proportions of those populations, but in general they are produced by the same capitalist system. While there is stark material inequality between developed and developing worlds and the struggle for basic survival faced by nearly half of the world's population requires drastic change, the developed world, and especially the Anglophone portions of it, is experiencing a mental-health crisis of enormous proportions. Even well before the point of identifiable mental illness, the need for an alternative way to feel, addressed so effectively by the social media timeline, is driven by the fact that many of us do not feel great about our lives, the world, or the future. We are measured, compared, blamed for our own problems, and pressured to compete according to terms on which we cannot "win," all while our sense of a bright future and a clear path towards it is taken away by political, economic, and even ecological factors beyond our control. What results is a feeling of emptiness, uncertainty, stagnation, and fear that can only ever be blocked out or escaped from by participating in various forms of enjoyment and consumption, which the corporations of the developed world are only too happy to provide. Capitalism has become established as a culture to which there is no alternative, and from which there is no escape, except subjectively and momentarily via consumption. Social media, as businesses themselves that feed on our need to be distracted from this system, are the most faithful manifestation of this system of all.

Thus social media use is primarily a pattern of compensatory media consumption that is both produced by broader patterns of capitalist life, and increasingly exploited by specific businesses such as Facebook Inc. While our usage is not beneficial to us in the long term at all, our affect-driven use of it for fleeting, compensatory reasons is of extreme commercial value to companies that are essentially exploiting the way that life within capitalist realism makes us feel. Social media corporations, and Facebook especially, have made gigantic and lucrative businesses based on positioning themselves between users and aspects of users' lives that in their original form might have provided some antidote to their unhappiness, such as friends, comforting food, relationships, events such as birthdays and holidays, novelty, and entertainment. Such architectures allow the capture of data about exactly what is meaningful and important to each user, which both provides a saleable commodity in the form of marketing data, and allows social networks to make themselves increasingly indispensable in the day-to-day emotional life of the user and to pass on the commercial value of this proximity to their advertisers. As we scroll through the timeline, desperate to be distracted and emotionally stimulated, we are almost trapped in a virtual hamster wheel of media consumption and data generation. Our reliance on emotionally distracting media to fill in the emptiness that capitalism makes many of us feel, in other words, is therefore being exploited by a generation of media businesses more ruthless and more effective than any before it.

In the first chapter of this book, I outlined some of the more worrying aspects of how using social media can affect us, from making us more depressed, jealous of others, or dissatisfied with our lives, to keeping us awake. These are not the only consequences however. Many other writers and researchers, from Evgeny Morozov to Jaron Lanier, have warned us about how an overreliance on social media may harm us, our societies, and even our democracies. There are two dimensions of the widespread use of social media — with all the hedonic media consumption, emotion regulation, mediation, and exploitation I have discussed — to which I would like to draw attention.

The first aspect of our relationship to social media that is problematic is the relinquishment of control over those media. As a matter of principle, it cannot be ignored that Facebook and other social networks are private, and especially that, as publicly-listed companies, they are owned by precisely the forms of capital that are implicated in making us unhappy to begin with. When our journalism, our sociality, our political commentary, our creativity, and a growing number of other aspects of our society are being permanently recorded for commercial gain in ways that we cannot access except as momentary consumers, we should be very cautious about meekly going along with this arrangement. As we will see, there are practical consequences in how this control is exercised over our media.

The second aspect of routine social media use that we should be careful about relates to information, or the lack of it, since most users' priorities are driven by emotion rather than the pursuit of information. As the world experiences an epidemic of ignorance, and the digital ecosystem shifts to what pundits are calling "post-factual," the flows of information and entertainment become confused as the drive to "fill the void" gets stronger. Using a hedonic, consumptive entertainment platform for our news and self-education is a dangerous and worrying development because it accommodates so easily the increasing *information resistance* of late-capitalist public spheres.

Both of these issues need to be understood thoroughly, and then fought against tirelessly. This chapter investigates these tendencies.

* * *

I. Enclosure, media alienation, memory, and imposed politics

We don't have a technology problem, we have a social problem.

Sir Tim Berners-Lee

Concerning situations arise when we allow any company in search of profit to mediate as much of our reality as social media platforms have been allowed to. Perhaps, allowing so much of what is important to us — our culture, entertainment, personal relationships, and even our own identities — to be mediated by a private company for their own commercial gain is something that we will look back on and wonder how on earth we let it happen. Even if birthdays aren't your thing, the conversion of birthdays from something that happens every year to something that happens every year on Facebook is one that we should resist on political grounds alone — these things belong to us, not Facebook.

When Mark Zuckerberg and his wife Priscilla Chan shared news of their pregnancy and three prior miscarriages on Facebook, it could only be interpreted as a subtle demonstration of how we are all meant to use Facebook — to share our intimate and personal stories with each other — but we should be cautious before following their example. Even if you genuinely found their story heart-warming or personal, as many people did, remember that the subtext of this communication was an encouragement that we feel more able to share such details of our own lives. Surely, Facebook will have hoped its users would think: If the founder of Facebook is doing this, it *must* be safe, so we can do it too? Mark Zuckerberg owns 28.2% of Facebook — by far the largest stake owned by anybody. Even if his data *are* sold to advertisers along with everybody else's, which is far from guaranteed, he still benefits from that sale and you don't. If he and his wife have managed to conceive, and that's what they want, then genuine congratulations to them, but the prominence of this information on Facebook is not as much of an unqualified reason to celebrate as the information itself. Never mind how it must have made couples feel who have been less fortunate, it is essentially an ad, and like much of Facebook, a means to make money from you.

Social media as enclosure

Enclosure is the process by which something that was formerly public, and shared by everybody, becomes private property. As Peter Linebaugh (2009) has written, enclosure is a fundamental aspect of how capitalism has operated since its earliest beginnings. One day a forest or a field would be common land, usable by everybody for any reasonable purpose, but swiftly it could be enclosed behind a fence, ending the activities that people had commonly partaken in there. Use of the land would continue, but only for the specific people and in the specific ways that the new "owners" of the land permitted. A free, shared resource suddenly became privately controlled. The opposing idea to enclosure — that of the *commons* — has often been used as a metaphor for digital culture. Legal scholar and former US presidential hopeful Lawrence Lessig has urged this view as an alternative to the strict system of copyright, and founded a popular and widely used system of alternative content-licensing known as *creative commons*. For most of human history, Lessig has argued, culture has been "read-write" in the sense that anybody could borrow or incorporate any idea and build on it. Certainly in folk traditions this is often still the case. With the stricter enforcement of copyright that became commonplace in the twentieth century, Lessig has argued, we transitioned to "read-only" culture, in which culture had to be bought, usually from large corporations, and could not be changed, incorporated into new creativity, or to use Lessig's word, "remixed." Lessig's view of the digital commons was that digitally-based cultures needed to be freed from these constraints so that they could return to being "read-write" cultures that could simultaneously support creative people's livelihoods while enabling remixing. The old idea of the commons was, in effect, *remixed* to become a radical argument about the future of our culture in relation to computers.

The corresponding idea of *enclosure*, however, is a less common metaphor in the discussion of our relation to digital capital, but it too needs to be revived. Rob Coley and Dean Lockwood have argued provocatively that the transfer of our culture to the all-storing, zero-friction, capitalism-friendly "Cloud" represents a form of enclosure. The cloud, however, is mostly an architecture of storage, access to that storage, and transfer via that storage. Social media platforms, by contrast, contain an interactive, constantly updating repository that is accessible at almost any moment via a user interface and with which many of their users tend to have a strangely intimate relationship

— more than they often realise. As I have outlined in the previous chapter however, these platforms are also a ruthless means to extract value from the subjective vulnerabilities of their users, and while they feel like free services full of commonly-owned culture, they are not.

There are two intertwined senses in which social networks amount to a metaphorical enclosure of the aspects of life that come into contact with them, in the same spirit as that described by Linebaugh. Firstly, as described in the previous chapter, they have become increasingly general as they have sought to mediate more and more aspects of our lives, swallowing up any area that is emotionally meaningful in order to harness that emotion for commercial purposes. In *becoming* birthdays, to use the example from the last chapter, they enclose birthdays; but in *becoming* friendships, anniversaries, entertainment, escape, distraction, and so forth, they enclose these areas of life too. Being "social" media points to an enclosure of sociality itself. Judging by its ad campaigns, Facebook Inc. wants all friendship to be conducted and mediated by its platform.

The second sense in which social networks represent enclosure is in relation to the media and culture that its users upload there, and it is this sense that requires fuller exploration below. Contrary to the popular belief that when you put photos or other media on Facebook the ownership of the intellectual property of that media is transferred to them, you continue to "own" the media you upload. I wrap the word "own" in quotation marks here, however, because the terms and conditions of usage that you agree to every time you use Facebook, Instagram, Twitter, or most other social media platforms makes this remaining "ownership" pretty meaningless in relation to how these platforms can treat your content. They are a clever way of avoiding backlash. In 2011, image-sharing site Lockerz, now largely superseded by Twitter's own image-sharing functionality, was found to be using the terms and conditions to transfer ownership outright. Twitpic, a similar service, was forced to change its terms and conditions because the platform forbade images that were hosted there from being sold to any third party, such as news agencies. In both cases, the terms of use were later updated to eliminate these provisions and resemble those of pretty much every other social network's terms and conditions in respect to intellectual property: You technically "own" your media at law but you guarantee us a worldwide, indefinite license to do what we want with your media. In the previous chapter, Instagram's changes to its terms and conditions to allow explicitly their sale of your media without your knowledge told a similar story.

Especially in an age where nobody actually reads the terms and conditions, uploading meaningful aspects of your life to a digital platform necessarily means surrendering aspects of control over those media. While a user's intentions may point in one direction, it is almost never the same direction as the cold, hard profits that social media corporations are anticipating. That means that any loss of control over your media in the context of your relationship to these enterprises creates potential that these media are essentially misused. French literary critic Roland Barthes argued in "The Death of the Author" that the age in which the author was the primary authority on the meaning of their work should come to an end. On social media, the age in which we have the primary authority over the media we create has similarly come to an end — "the death of the uploader," one could call it in pseudo-Barthesian terms. On Facebook, the only way to destroy their control over your media is to destroy your media themselves by deleting them from Facebook. Given the emotional importance of this content and the reactions it has elicited such as comments and "likes," this is the equivalent of asking somebody to burn down their house to stop the bank from owning it. It is hard to watch some friends uploading images of their young children and other media that capture important or intimate moments in their lives without being reminded of how they are quietly being alienated from their own pictures. Some users are aware that in sharing media on social media platforms they are licensing their content potentially to be used commercially by strangers for unspecified purposes, but the balance of priorities makes sharing more important. The majority however, are more focused on the act of sharing itself.

Loss of control

Not only does sharing these media on social networks enclose them by bringing them to a private platform over which we have no further influence; the conflicting intentions around such content-sharing also encloses and alienates us from each other. In September 2016 it was reported that an unnamed Austrian teenager was suing her parents for posting embarrassing baby pictures of her on Facebook, which they refused to remove. The young woman had not discovered the images until she joined Facebook, some three years after the images had been posted. "They knew no shame or limits," she told Austria's *Die ganze Woche* magazine, as reported in the *Irish Times*. "Whether I was sitting on the potty or naked in my crib, my every step was recorded photographically and, afterwards, made public." The *Irish Times* reports that German law already makes it possible for teenagers from the age of fourteen and up to use the courts to make their parents remove content from social-network sites, and French law provides for a forty-five thousand euro fine or even prison for parents who upload embarrassing pictures of their children.

Even if the media shared are not personal or emotionally important, there is a broader picture of this enclosure that should be concerning in principle even if it has less practical impact. Memes, pictures of kittens or cake, videos of varying descriptions, and other media, whoever made them, and for whatever reason, are all covered by the same license. Whatever our impulses, or the messages we intend to communicate in the media we share, the fact of their immediately being licensed instantly to a large, multinational corporation is not nothing, and should at the very least be a conscious part of our thinking. Anybody who would be unhappy about walking into a corporate boardroom with a USB stick containing an unpublished novel, an album of home-recorded songs, or baby pictures of their child and saying to the assembled executives as they slide it over the table: "Here guys, use these for whatever you like," should consider that sharing such images on Facebook or other social media, as opposed to via email or some other private medium, is virtually the same in its implications for those materials. When Tim Berners-Lee announced the "world wide web" in 1991, the underlying HTML format it used was an open medium that anybody could use for any purpose, free of charge, and this commons-like approach was what built the early web. Despite the internet's military history, the open standard of HTML was, in some senses, "the People's medium." Placing our culture and our digital lives within a privatised infrastructure is a drastic departure from this model, however. How can we let this happen to our culture itself; to our public sphere? The subjective motivations are understandable, but the overall outcome is still as ethically dubious as enclosure always has been.

Remembering what is best forgotten

The problems with allowing our culture to be enclosed, however, do not stop there. In the 1700s, Brazilian explorers deep in the rainforest of northwestern Brazil encountered a tribe called the Pirahã. The culture of this tribe is so unusual that, for example, some linguists think their language refutes the laws of language discovered by linguist Noam Chomsky that otherwise account adequately for every known human language on Earth. Another aspect of Pirahã culture that appears to be unique is how the experience of time is constructed. The Pirahã do not *remember* or make meaning out of memory or abstract symbols of things that have been or will be.

According to linguist Dan Everett, reported in the *New Yorker*, Pirahã language has "no numbers, no fixed color terms, no perfect tense, no deep memory, no tradition of art or drawing, and no words for 'all,' 'each,' 'every,' 'most,' or 'few.'" Their culture reportedly "has no collective memory that extends back more than one or two generations, and no original creation myths." The relationship between their language and their experience of time is of course reminiscent of French psychiatrist Jacques Lacan's argument that the experience of time and of things having an identity over time is an effect of language that structures time in this way. At any rate, the Pirahã are interesting because as a culture they do not seek to remember everything or create a history; they seem odd precisely because most other cultures, including that of postmodern late capitalism, seek to remember so much.

I have already described in Chapter Two the timeline's orientation around abundant, distracting novelty, as the user scrolls further and further down in rough reverse-chronological order; I have also outlined in Chapter Three how late-capitalist working conditions often reduce what Judy Wajcman has called "time sovereignty"; and I have discussed in Chapter Four the ways that social media, like much of capitalism, seeks to make itself memorable to us by becoming the important events such as birthdays, Christmases, New Years, and more unusual events too. Here we can observe yet another aspect of how time structures our culture, and how this is reflected in social networks. In comparison to the Pirahã, we seem to be obsessed with remembering everything. The fact that Facebook stores every event, be it the posting of a photo or the addition of a "friend," as something that can have an "anniversary" years later is the expression of a specific cultural feature that should not necessarily be welcome in the architecture of social media platforms.

In *Delete*, Viktor Mayer-Schönberger has urged that in a digital age, the capacity to forget is both virtuous and necessary (2011). He cites a number of examples of individuals whose innocent, private moments became incorporated into social media in various ways, both with and without their consent, and who paid enormous consequences as a result. The consequences are not always predictable, but like the young Austrian woman suing her parents, they often have privacy consequences. When nurse Rebecca Leighton was wrongly accused of murdering five people in Stepping Hill hospital in Manchester, the press plundered her Facebook past, using pictures of her drinking and fooling about with her friends as evidence of her moral inferiority and likely culpability. A quick search for her name in Google Images shows that most of these images are still publicly accessible years later.

Shakespeare scholar Emma Smith has also argued that "we need to remember how to forget," calling the insistence on remembering everything *hyperthymesis*. "Memory has become prosthetic – outsourced to the internet, to external hard drive or cloud storage system. What should we remember? What should be preserved? The paradox of the digital future is the burden of the past that we are constantly archiving," she says (2016).

Writing as a person of unusually accurate memory, I can attest that when people consider me to have inappropriately remembered too much, however innocently I might have done so, they seem to find it strange or even creepy. So why are we so happy for social media platforms to record everything that happens there in perfect detail in a database to which ultimately we have no direct access? As a technology, the database is of highly dubious origins, one of its first applications having been to keep track of concentration-camp inmates in Nazi Germany (Black, 2012). The insistence of digital capitalism on remembering everything about us, and particularly the ways in which social media platforms use our vulnerabilities to incorporate us into the enclosure of our own pasts, is something that needs to be subjected to far more scrutiny and critique at the very least. I suspect if more people saw it this way, it would quickly decline.

Politicised constructions of reality

Another serious issue with the way that social networks enclose meaningful and important aspects of our lives is the effect they may have on the content or information that they mediate in doing so, both inadvertently and deliberately. I have repeatedly said that technology reflects, rather than determines, our culture or behaviour. When Marshall McLuhan argued that "the medium is the message," this was an erroneous and highly deterministic position. This doesn't mean, however, that a technology designed and created by people with specific cultures, ideas, and motives, such as profit, can't enable and encourage behaviours and political subjectivities over time — altering the meaning of the aspects of our culture that become filtered through that technology. Networks such as Facebook and Twitter are designed and built by human beings, mostly American, mostly white, mostly male, and mostly in California, who have a culturally-specific subjective relation to the media and culture for which their technologies have become the conduit, and who will inevitably build their platforms according to this outlook. At all times we should be asking ourselves: Does the way I use this technology, the way it has been designed, and/or the way it is operated, change the way I think about the areas of life to which it relates? Is what I see subtly cheapened, overvalued, or distorted by the medium? When, as with social media, technology can come to relate to so many areas of our lives, these questions should be constant, and posed with every use.

Is Facebook's idea of a meaningful birthday the same as yours? Once your birthdays are an annual occurrence that is incomplete without Facebook, will you remember what birthdays were like before they were absorbed onto it? As I have alluded to, birthdays are clearly different in an era of mobile phones, emails, and digital cameras than they were before these technologies, not because the technologies themselves made them different but because Western capitalist culture wanted them to be different and the technologies allowed this. But birthdays are too simple of an example to show fully why this is such a problem, so let's consider some more complex, if commonplace, cases.

Echoing Lawrence Lessig's work nearly a decade earlier, Rebecca MacKinnon (2012) reminds us that "Internet and telecommunications companies […] create computer code that functions as a kind of law, in that it shapes what people can do and sometimes directly censors what they can see." Whereas the storage and perfect recall of events in our lives, as described above, can be problematic, the loss of control over our media can also be manifested by the reverse situation: Sometimes Facebook and other platforms want us to forget things that should be remembered.

On July 6th 2016 in Falcon Heights, St. Paul, Minnesota, against a backdrop of regular police shootings of African Americans and considerable public anger in response, officer Jeronimo Yanez fatally shot thirty-two year-old Philando Castile as he sat in his car after a tense exchange of words. Also in the car were Castile's girlfriend, Diamond Reynolds, and her four year-old daughter. In the moments immediately following the shooting, Reynolds began live-streaming video of still-alive Castile, who was slumped in the driver's seat of the car, and of her exchanges with the officer. "Lord please Jesus don't tell me that he's gone. Please don't tell me that he's gone. Please officer, don't tell me that you just did this to him. You shot four bullets into him, sir. He was just getting his license and registration, sir," Reynolds can be heard saying in the video. As technology website *The Next Web* reported the following day, "Roughly one hour after the video went live, the content mysteriously disappeared from the social network. Reynolds' Facebook profile was also temporarily removed." Widespread accusations of censorship and of deleting the evidence of a crime began almost immediately. *The Next Web* reported that "In a statement to *TechCrunch*, Facebook said the removal was due to a technical glitch and the video was restored about an hour after it went down, resurfacing with a graphic content warning."

Ok, an innocent mistake, one could say — the suggestion that Facebook's content policies are aligned to the USA's structures of power and enforcement is perhaps too much, for some. We'll never know why Facebook actually deleted the video, whether it was an accidental "glitch" or gung-ho censorship that was reversed in response to public outcry. *The Register* reports that its deletion was demanded by law enforcement: "Multiple sources have told *The Register* that police removed video footage of Castile's death from Facebook, potentially tampering with evidence."

The same thing happened when twenty-three year-old Korryn Gaines was killed by police after a five-hour standoff, having posted videos to Facebook of various moments during the confrontation. Her Facebook and Instagram profiles were deleted, along with the videos they contained. This time, the request from law enforcement was made explicit.

Such deletion is not isolated to confrontations between US citizens and the police. Arabic-language Facebook pages *Quds* and *Shehab News Agency*, with five million and six million "likes" respectively, exclusively provide information about the Israel/Palestine conflict. Editorially they are largely sympathetic to the injustice suffered by Palestinians, and tend to focus on the actions of the Israeli government, but they are also critical of the Palestinian government at times. In late September 2016, the administrators of both pages found that their Facebook accounts had been suspended without warning. The following day, Facebook reinstated their accounts, telling Palestine-focused news website *Electronic Intifada*: "The pages were removed in error and restored as soon as we were able to investigate [...] Our team processes millions of reports each week, and we sometimes get things wrong. We're very sorry about this mistake." Again, as with the cases above in the United States, we may say: Fair enough, an innocent mistake. Yet again, however, this would be a somewhat naïve belief and incredulity about these Facebook account suspensions being a mere accident would not be unfounded. In the US, sympathy for the Palestinians is seldom featured in mainstream media, and is politically indigestible in mainstream corridors of politics, largely due to the efforts of powerful pro-Israel lobbies. US politicians aspiring to any office must line up and offer unqualified support for Israel in order to be elected. In October 2016 Pink Floyd singer Roger Waters lost a major sponsorship deal with American Express for his 2017 US+Them tour because of his support for students in California who were organising for the Boycott Divest & Sanctions (BDS) campaign against the Israeli occupation.

Against this backdrop it is already difficult to see Facebook's interventions as accidental, but it gets worse — only days before the users' accounts were suspended, on September 12th 2016, Associated Press reported that Facebook had openly begun working with members of the Israeli government to censor content that was critical of Israel. The stated reasons for this intervention are that it would be in order to counter online "hate speech," and the violence that is said to result from it. Genuine hate speech and violence are obviously to be condemned outright, irrespective of whom they are directed at or what the political context may be, and there is undoubtedly a problem of vile anti-Semitic abuse amongst the abhorrent racism and bigotry that flows more generally across social media platforms from Facebook to Twitter to Reddit. Nevertheless there are reasons to believe that in this case it may be a bit more complicated than simply stopping hate speech. The Israeli government has been using social media posts to investigate those promoting the BDS movement that seeks to challenge Israeli policy with non-violent tactics, ever since the overt support of BDS was made illegal in Israel in 2011. Political speech about Israel is broadly monitored by the Israeli government, and according to investigative news website *The Intercept*, Israel has "begun actively surveilling Palestinians for the content of their Facebook posts and even arresting some for clear political speech." In May 2016, for example, makeup artist Nidal Atwan was jailed for forty-five days and fined eight hundred dollars for injudicious comments she had made about a recent bus bombing. According to website *Samidoun*, astrophysics professor Dr Imad Barghouthi was sentenced in October 2016 to seven months in jail and a five-hundred-dollar fine "for posting about Palestinian politics and occupation on Facebook and social media." *Al Jazeera* reports that Israel has detained or jailed approximately a hundred and fifty Palestinians for things they have said on Facebook since October 2015.

Ultimately, one might point out that these are the standard authoritarian actions of a government that feels threatened by political conversations online, as described by Evgeny Morozov and others, even if Israel is better at appearing to be a liberal democracy with freedom of expression than, say, China or Russia. This is hardly Facebook's fault, you could say, and has nothing to do with "filling the void." Surely, as long as online social platforms concentrate on responding objectively to the more serious moral transgressions like "hate speech," the only political censorship will come from governments, as it always does? The difficult thing about that argument, however, is the way in which Facebook, or any other social network, can be quietly manipulated into towing the line and serving a political agenda while appearing to be neutral. They can be made to sway arguments in one direction or another. In the case of Facebook's collaboration with Israel, there is a stark double-standard that has become intrinsic to the way conversations about Israel are controlled on Facebook, and that illustrates the worrying lack of accountability that Facebook and others are subjected to when they become the go-to platform for our political discussions. Members of the same Israeli government that have insisted that Facebook crack down on "hate speech" on Facebook, as well as outlawed entirely non-violent calls for BDS, are themselves guilty of very similar-looking hate speech — against Palestinians — without any repercussions at all, from Facebook's censors or otherwise: In June 2014 for example, *Al Jazeera* reports that "Israeli lawmaker Ayelet Shaked published a status on Facebook [which she subsequently deleted] declaring the 'entire Palestinian people as the enemy.'" *Electronic Intifada* reports that her post "was shared more than one thousand times and received almost five thousand 'Likes.'" What we see here is that on the one hand, Israeli politicians are insisting (successfully) that Facebook deletes content to crack down on what they determine to be hate speech, whilst at the same moment they themselves are guilty of the very same transgression, albeit with the balance of political power squarely on their side. Similar utterances are either sanctioned or not, purely by virtue of which side of the dispute they happen to fall on and who wields the power to influence their censorship, and in the end we see that it has far more to do with suppressing criticism of Israel than controlling hate speech.

Whether the imposition of this double-standard onto Facebook's users is internal, is imposed from outside, or both — whether you think the erasures described above are truly accidental misfirings of some algorithm, routine due process of law, or effectively an editorial policy — the picture they reveal is ultimately a damning one. It shows that to embrace for-profit corporations such as Facebook as the de-facto home of political speech is to entrust these important political conversations to companies that will comply with whichever political power (or invisible financial pressure) is most prudently appeased. From a panic-stricken car in St. Paul, Minnesota, to a house in Bethlehem, occupied West Bank, one of the most worrying issues about our public sphere being enclosed within social media is when political or cultural subjectivity is imposed onto the content that is uploaded, in a way that users have little recourse to prevent.

As stated above, the provenance of networks such as Facebook and Twitter is mostly North American, white, and male, and as we have seen above, it is inescapable that the specific cultural subjectivity that these represent, both separately and together, would not be expressed in the workings of social media platforms. In the case of Facebook's censure of evidence of police brutality or its de-activation of the accounts of Palestinian activists, there has been outcry, largely due to the polarised, and highly political nature of the issues involved. The imposition of subjectivity doesn't only occur in relation to these types of issues, however. It can also occur more subtly and in more intimate, cultural areas of life, such as in gender relations and how these are expressed in the representation of our own bodies and those of others. Here too, it has been met with outcry.

As I have argued in Chapter Two, one of the primary functions of the timeline is emotional self-regulation and stimulation, and *arousal* in the broadest sense is an essential part of this subjective experience. As we have seen from the hedonic consumption of "food porn" and so forth, Facebook and Instagram's businesses are dependent on making distinctions between what are acceptable stimuli for arousal and what are not, getting the line between taboo and acceptability as close as possible to taboo enjoyment without actually leaving the realm of social acceptability or revealing their strategy.

The history of taboo around the human body, and particularly in relation to its sexual functions, is as old as culture itself, and yet this subjectivity is not always manifested in outright censorship. Instead, cultures have often responded by enclosing sexual taboos in specific cultural forms, often controlled by men. As art critic and theorist John Berger (1990) reminds us, depictions of women dominate one category of European painting more than any other — the nude — and Americans spend 13.1 billion dollars on pornography every year. As always, there is little reason why we shouldn't expect the same cultural features to extend into our use of the web, and Ethan Zuckerman (2008) has gone so far as to argue that the appearance of pornography on any digital platform is the first sign that it is functional enough for everyday use: "Porn is a weak test for the success of participatory media – it's like tapping a mike and asking, 'Is it on?' If you're not getting porn in your system, it doesn't work." In a way, this is quite an admission.

Let us not forget that Facebook's own provenance was originally as *Facemash*, a means of comparing people's "hotness," which fell just on the wrong side of that threshold and nearly got Mark Zuckerberg kicked out of Harvard (Kirkpatrick, 2010). As a means to avoid revealing this provenance, social networks have tended to embrace the other, puritanical extreme instead — Facebook's internal censorship guide is even referred to informally as "the bible" (Webster, 2012). However, like Queen Gertrude, Hamlet's mother, said upon seeing her guilty self represented in a play, they "doth protest too much, methinks." The consequence is a patriarchal, controlling, automatic sexualisation of the female body.

Female nipples, according to the enforced content guidelines of Facebook and Instagram, seem to be inherently sexual, and until recently were completely banned on Facebook, even in cases where the picture obviously depicted a mother breastfeeding or some other patently non-sexual scenario. In October 2016, Facebook removed a campaign video about breast cancer by the Swedish Cancer Society, despite the video being entirely comprised of cartoon animation, and featuring pink circles to represent the breasts of the women in the video, who were showing the viewer how to check for lumps. Facebook apologised, telling the BBC "We're very sorry, our team processes millions of advertising images each week, and in some instances we incorrectly prohibit ads." This sounds awfully familiar to Facebook's other apologies, above. In January 2016, a woman named Rowena Kincaid, incidentally a former picture editor for the BBC, posted a picture of a rash on her breast that was a readily identifiable symptom of the stage four breast cancer she had been diagnosed with some years earlier, in a bid to motivate others with the same symptoms to seek treatment. Facebook censored (i.e. removed) the close-up image of her breast because it happened to include the nipple, but later reinstated it claiming that "In this instance we made a mistake and have reinstated the photograph." Again, an ever-so-innocent apology, but no recognition of the wider pattern of which these apologies are a regular part. Kincaid, who died in September 2016 after a seven-year battle with cancer, told the *Independent* that

"I wasn't out to offend anyone. [The picture] looks like something out of a medical journal.", Conversely, when breast cancer left a woman named Alison Habbal without a nipple on one breast, she was able to circumvent these rules and share an image of an ornate tattoo she had received in that area of her body without being censored beyond the obfuscation that the tattoo had already provided. This latter case is somewhat surprising, given the hysteria and hyper-sexualisation that has frequently been imposed on how women represent themselves: It would be easy to imagine a situation in which the image was censored anyway, despite the image not technically meeting the "nipple" criterion for censorship. The narrow preoccupation with women's breasts and especially nipples as some sort of watershed for digital content is at once bizarre and entirely predictable given both the breast's sexualisation, and the psychoanalytical significance of the breast as a site of comfort and pleasure for nursing children (Yalom, 1997). But this kind of technical ontology for what the "community" should be expected to tolerate is not always quite so stubbornly fixed on specific signifiers, and images are indeed censored for their content alone. In March 2015, artist Rupi Kaur's posts, which subtly depicted, according to the *Daily Telegraph*, a "fully clothed woman lying in bed with a period stain behind her," were deleted — *twice*. Instagram's "Community Guidelines" "prohibit sexual acts, violence and nudity – they do not mention anything about periods," the *Telegraph* reports.

In another example, from September 2016, Norwegian writer Tom Egeland posted an article on Facebook entitled "Seven photographs that changed the history of warfare," accompanied by the seven photographs. One of these images was the iconic "napalm girl" photo taken by Nick Ut in 1972 that showed several children including a naked Phan Thi Kim Phúc — then a nine year-old girl — escaping from a napalm attack. Egeland's account was promptly suspended. According to the *Guardian*, when Egeland's newspaper *Aftenposten* disclosed publicly that this had happened, they were contacted by Facebook with a message stating that "Any photographs of people displaying fully nude genitalia or buttocks, or fully nude female breast, will be removed," and asking that they "either remove or pixelize" the image. Before they could do this, however, Facebook deleted the post altogether. After a few days, and major public outcry, Facebook eventually backed down, stating that "While we recognize that this photo is iconic, it's difficult to create a distinction between allowing a photograph of a nude child in one instance and not others."

Fear about sexual imagery taking over the web is as old as the web itself. In 1993, for example, the inventor of the World Wide Web Sir Tim Berners-Lee was reportedly against the implementation of inline images on web pages because, somewhat prophetically, he feared people would post too much pornography. More than two decades later, the same debate is ongoing. Content enforcement on Instagram, for example, is reportedly a game of constant cat-and-mouse, and there are said to be more than a million pornographic images on the platform, often hidden under hashtags that use Arabic script, accented characters, suggestive-looking emojis and other means to avoid Anglophone control systems (Khalid, 2016).

This is not to say that it would be better not to implement any controls on content. As the work of psychologist Gary Wilson (2015) and others has shown, consumption of sexually explicit materials can sometimes be detrimental, especially to young people, and the internet greatly facilitates this access. Rather, the point is that the very form of media consumption that social media entail, the ways they are used, the economic relationships that they comprise (as outlined in Chapter Four), and the way that these intersect with political and social issues are all fundamentally flawed. Facebook is, after all, a company that has no compunction about allowing advertisers to target only white people (Angwin & Parris, 2016). The issue is not so much the presence or absence of sexually explicit material, but that as with the question of what is "hate speech" or what is evidence of police brutality, the question of what is or is not sexual about the body cannot be entrusted to commercial, unaccountable organisations whose main priorities are their own profits and share price. The hegemonic reassertion of specific cultural subjectivities, and even downright prejudice, is virtually inevitable.

We know from Noam Chomsky and Edward Herman's political critique of the mass media *Manufacturing Consent* (1988) that media ownership matters, and has implications for the use of media to challenge hegemonic power structures. Who owns the media we rely on to learn about the world has always had an influence on what we are allowed to learn about, and how we perceive the aspects of the world that are signified by those media. Whether it is removing evidence of police murdering innocent citizens, censoring media sympathetic to the Palestinian cause, or insisting that we sexualise the naked — often female — body, the lack of control that we experience when our culture is enclosed into a private, commercial database is both a feature and a flaw.

As we desperately "fill the void" on social media, we are nonetheless encouraging and participating in exactly this process, effectively gifting our culture, our public sphere, and the emotions they elicit to the most sophisticated, manipulative, and yet unaccountable form of media ownership that we have ever seen. We should not be surprised when the representations they make with our culture turn out to favour those who hold power and influence.

* * *

II. After the fact: The problem of affective content, ignorance and democracy

All I know is what's on the internet.

Donald J. Trump

People in this country have had enough of experts.

Michael Gove

Some of these things are true and some of them lies. But they are all good stories.

Hilary Mantel, *Wolf Hall*

Americans appear to be losing touch with reality.

Thomas E. Patterson

The second worrying consequence of the "filling the void" pattern relates to the mixed usage of social media platforms. In Chapter Two, four essential qualities of the social media timeline were proposed that each enable and encourage this behaviour in different ways, combining to powerful effect. One of these features is especially relevant to the role of information and its consumption: the *mixture* of dramatically different forms of media content found in the timeline, including the juxtaposition of news and information with non-informational media. Broadly, I've argued that the main usage of the social media timeline is affect-driven; a form of hedonic media consumption that provides emotion regulation by means of distraction from, and compensation for, poor affect such as loneliness, distress and boredom. There is no denying, however, that some people do use social media to find out what is happening in a factual sense, and journalistic content does indeed also appear in the timeline, alongside the selfies, "listicles," memes and holiday snaps. According to a study by Pew Research Centre published in May 2016, 62% of US adults get some of their news via social media, and 18% do so often. Facebook even added a "trending" feature in 2014 that organised media related to current topics in a way that was easier to browse. The question is: are these two areas of usage compatible? If you are looking for information about the world via the same means that you "fill the void", might these ontologically distinct uses not become dangerously "blurred and often difficult to tell apart" as Natalie Fenton (2012) has argued?

Since social media are often said to be the cause of misinformation, it is worth saying something initially about the status of "information" generally — particularly that of a political or civic nature. Journalists have long held that the "right to know" is the cornerstone of democracy, and according to a qualitative study of the professional epistemology of journalists by media sociologist Mark Deuze (2005), journalists consider themselves an essential service that provides the public with exactly this information. Besides the somewhat out-dated positivism about "knowledge" and objective "truth," the problem here is that audiences may no longer consider the provision of information as such an intrinsically valuable service. As Adam Curtis has alluded to in his 2016 film *HyperNormalisation*, in a postmodern, neoliberalised world where it has become impossible for most people to be sure of what is fact and what is not, enlightenment concepts such as the "truth" are overused and overemphasised to the point they are meaningless and cease to have the currency they once had. Consequently, people have begun to seek out information less and less, instead preferring entertainment and other distractions as a vain attempt to bolster their emotional survival. Affect and belief have increasingly come to dominate, and people tend settle on whichever speculations or narratives will justify their existing subjectivities.

The situation that results from this development has increasingly been labeled as "post-factual" or "post truth". A looser relationship to empirically oriented forms of "truth" is nothing new, but it is important that in each instance we understand its provenance, particularly where technology is said to be responsible.

Philosopher Hannah Arendt argued in *The Origins of Totalitarianism* (1951) that:

> The ideal subject of totalitarian rule is not the convinced Nazi or the convinced Communist, but people for whom the distinction between fact and fiction (i.e., the reality of experience) and the distinction between true and false (i.e., the standards of thought) no longer exist.

Whatever the reader may or may not feel about Arendt's overall political persuasions, these words also ring truer than ever, more than sixty years later, for the "ideal" subject of late capitalism — an informational landscape that not only encourages and rewards this more complicated relationship with information, but often requires it. Political media scholars Natalie Fenton (2012), Thomas E. Patterson (2010), and Markus Prior (2007) have all written of how an abundance of media that are in some way more appealing than news and information can lead to "information inequality". To understand such a situation as a form of inequality is instructive, and is more than a simple metaphor. Just like material and social forms of inequality, information inequality has the tendency to worsen over time. Patterson has said that:

> A consequence is that the knowledge gap between the more informed and the less informed is expanding. In today's high-choice media environment, the less informed opt for entertainment programming while the more informed include the news junkies.

Another respect in which information inequality is like other forms of inequality required by capitalism is how it exploits those who have less, encouraging and then feeding on ignorance. This happens in a number of ways. To start with, as stated in the opening chapter of this book, there is the sheer degree to which those in the (over)developed world have become complicit in things they don't agree with. When people are confronted with the idea that they are implicated in making worse the very elements of the world or of their own lives that they perceive to be problematic or scary, or that they are contradictory in some other way, they feel undermined and seek alternative analyses that avoid such contradictions, even if they are far-fetched. With man-made climate change for example, it is much easier to drive an SUV, eat beef and dairy products, and travel by air regularly, if you decide that carbon emissions have no impact, and that the vast majority of climate scientists who say otherwise are either wrong, or perpetrating a global conspiracy to suppress the emission of greenhouse gases. The same pattern of wilful, consumption-driven ignorance exists in other areas too: sweatshop labour, harmful food additives, crop-driven deforestation such as that for palm oil or soya, and the raw material supply chains for electronic components.

A second factor leading to information-aversive media consumption and information inequality is that the sources that were once trusted and considered authoritative — particularly government and the mainstream press — have lost much of their credibility, as their firm, deceptive loyalty to entrenched power and capital has been slowly revealed. It is a common occurrence to hear people from nearly any part of the political spectrum say that the media are "biased," and regardless of the subjectivities that give way to that feeling, it is often true — even if not in the ways alleged. As Edward Herman and Noam Chomsky argued in *Manufacturing Consent*, the mass media all-too-often prioritise the interests of the wealthy elite by whom they are usually owned and sometimes subsidised (1988). Journalism's increasing reliance on advertising, as its other revenue streams have declined, only exacerbates this problem.

Finally, there has been a catastrophic breakdown in the way people are educated. A neoliberal, late-capitalist education system is increasingly one that teaches people to function, and to perform at ever-higher levels, but not necessarily to think critically. It emphasises standardised testing and stresses "delivery" over enquiry; "resilience" over versatility. While ever-greater numbers of people go to university, universities themselves continue to be mercilessly reconfigured around the rules of the market. Even going to university is by no means accessible to all. A 2016 study found that the decreasing availability of need-based financial support for undergraduate education in the US meant decreased degree completion rates (Goldrick-Rab et al., 2016). The "right to know" is not only disappearing from journalism; it is disappearing from education too.

From our participation as consumers in ways that are detrimental to our own long-term interests, to our media outlets' deference to a status quo that is highly unequal in the balance of power, to the destruction of education according to market rules, it would seem that entrenched structures of power and capital are at the roots of information inequality in a variety of different ways, and capital is usually the primary beneficiary too.

More concerning still are the effects of a post-factual relationship between people and their media. If verifiable information is optional while socially-driven communication and affect are essential, it is both easier and more pleasant to be ignorant. In a highly connected world this makes for a lethal combination that allows ignorance to grow and spread faster than ever, transforming the last vestigial aspects of democracy, such as elections and referenda, into vicious, destructive, polluting mob-rule. The combination of widespread anger, misinformation and ignorance in relation to public matters such as the environment, or the political status of disempowered people is, at the time of writing, beginning to produce some high-profile outcomes. On the morning of June 24th 2016, people around the world woke up to find that the electorate of the United Kingdom had narrowly voted to leave the European Union in a bitterly fought referendum that had disrupted political conventions and alliances that were decades old. Four and a half months later, on the morning of November 9th, the world was forced to contend with the news that the people of the United States had elected infamous property tycoon and reality TV personality Donald Trump as president of the United States.

Whether events such as the British vote to leave the European Union and the election of Donald Trump were working-class rebellions against neoliberalism that have been horribly misdirected towards immigrants, or plain old nationalism and xenophobia, is a matter for other more qualified writers to determine and consider. Either way, both political events are inescapably born of widespread ignorance — sometimes wilful, sometimes enforced, and both have been forged in this "post-factual" scenario. In theory, elections and referenda are supposed to be fair, democratic exercises that allow important political agency and self-determination to be exercised by citizens themselves. The problem is that referenda, elections, and other democratic exercises only work when people actually have enough information on which to make an informed decision about how to vote, but this has been far from the case in both instances. According to the *Washington Post*, large numbers of people in Britain were googling "what is the eu" [sic] during and immediately after the EU vote (Fung, 2016). Many of the areas that had higher proportions of people who voted to leave the European Union were areas that benefitted most from EU funding (Cadwalladr, 2016). An ITV poll, taken more than three months after the vote, showed that the main reason by far that people in the UK voted to leave the European Union was so that the UK could set its own immigration policy and prevent the Freedom of Movement guaranteed by the EU treaties to citizens of member states, whom many voters believed to be causing overcrowding and placing a strain on public services. Despite the obvious racism in this belief, one of the other problems with it was that it was entirely inaccurate: EU migrants contributed a net benefit to the UK's public finances (O'Leary, 2016), and the overcrowding was largely due to austerity policies that had led to cuts in public services. A feature in the UK's *Telegraph* from May 2016, one month before the referendum, showed that membership of the UK Independence Party was highest in the areas with fewest immigrants (Dodds, 2015). Shortly after the vote, a man interviewed in the street in the South Yorkshire town of Barnsley told the *Huffington Post* that "it's all about immigration. It's to stop the Muslims from coming into this country. [...] The movement of people in Europe, fair enough, but not from Africa, Syria, Iraq, everywhere else." This was despite the fact that EU membership only affected the movement of citizens from other member states.

Similarly with Donald Trump's rise to power, ignorance — and all the prejudice and bigotry that tend to stem from it — were central features of that campaign. According to a May 2016 survey of registered US voters, 65% of Trump's supporters believed that Barack Obama was a Muslim, and 61% believed he was born outside of the United States — making him ineligible to be President. The expression of anti-immigrant sentiments was again a common trope, and Trump's claim that Mexicans arriving in the US were likely to be "rapists", for example, was widely reported. In the run-up to his emphatic victory, Trump — who had repeatedly declared he would forcibly remove millions of undocumented immigrants, and began the process of doing so once elected — told supporters at his rallies that were his opponent Hillary Clinton elected, she would allow more than six hundred million immigrants to enter the United States, tripling the country's population "in one week."

Theodor Adorno (1957) wrote of anti-Semitic propaganda in the USA in the early 1950s that:

> Fascist propaganda attacks bogies rather than real opponents, that is to say, it builds up an *imagery* of the Jew, or of the Communist, and tears it to pieces, without caring much how this imagery is related to reality.

As Primo Levi wrote in Italian newspaper *Corriere della Sera* in 1974, "Every era has its fascism." Upon reading Adorno's words it is hard not to be reminded of Trump's claims about Mexicans, Nigel Farage's characterisation of Eastern Europeans as more likely to claim benefits or be criminal, the widespread portrayal of Muslims as sympathetic to acts of terror, the racist cartoons of French magazine *Charlie Hebdo* or the vile billboards produced by the UK Independence Party to encourage people to vote to leave the European Union. All are undoubtedly instances of the same pathology.

Societies are far more vulnerable to the effects of malicious, racist, or wildly inaccurate media when they are not interested in their verification, yet such media are highly popular and this popularity only exacerbates their effects. *Fox News*, which once fought a lawsuit in Florida on the basis that the freedom of speech afforded under the First Amendment gave them the right to deliberately publish incorrect stories (Phillips, 2004), is the United States' most watched TV news (Gallup, Inc., 2013). UK newspaper *The Sun* is the country's most popular print newspaper (Press Gazette, 2015), despite publishing repeated and serious factual errors, such as the assertion that the European Court of Human Rights is an institution of the European Union, which any journalist writing about such matters should know is false (Wagner, 2014). The connection between these two outlets is not only that consumers tend to seek them because they will confirm how consumers already *feel*. The other connection is that they are both owned by companies controlled by right-wing Australian-American tycoon Rupert Murdoch. Murdoch tried to jump on the social media bandwagon too, and bought pre-Facebook social media platform MySpace in 2005. He was reportedly too focused on making money from the site, and sold it in 2011 after haemorrhaging both money and users, and being overtaken in terms of total users by Facebook in 2008 (Rushton, 2013).

The post-factual and social media

By now it should be clear that whatever the deterministic arguments out there, the conflation of fact and fiction and the preference for inaccurate media that accords with existing anger, outrage, and hatred is not in any way *caused* by, or unique to, social media or digital technology. Yet there are good reasons why such topics must be addressed in a book of which one unifying theme is social media. Whatever your opinion of Black Lives Matter, the British referendum on leaving the European Union, Donald Trump, Palestine, or global warming, you will appreciate that social media are frequently a means by which these types of heavily polarised public debates are taking place, largely because of their emotional import and capacity for arousal. This is particularly the case for younger people, perhaps because, as media commentator Geert Lovink (2012) has argued, "another consequence of Web 2.0 is that news media are, at best, secondary sources. [...] [F]or most young people 'old media' lost their legitimacy a long time ago."

"Web 2.0" was the positivist buzzword that referred to a web that was interactive, and which primarily featured content uploaded by other users. Media commentator Andrew Keen was largely dismissed as overly pessimistic when he characterised "web 2.0" as a "cult of the amateur" — a naïve obsession with the wisdom of "noble amateurs", that "[threatened] to turn our intellectual traditions and institutions upside down" (2008). Yet this view of the web now seems relatively palatable compared to how, a decade later, the "web 2.0" story has actually unfolded. Likewise, the famous *XKCD* cartoon in which one character is unable to go to bed because "somebody is wrong on the internet" seems awfully benign given how things have played out. Larger numbers of people than ever seem to be wrong on the internet. It has been said that "a lie can travel halfway around the world before the truth has got its boots on." In a delightfully ironic demonstration of exactly the unreliability of social media, this quote can be easily found misattributed to a variety of people, rendered in "word porn" form in elegant typography. Winston Churchill and Mark Twain both feature prominently as would-be authors of the quote, and it is frequently attributed to Twain in the year 1919, despite the fact that he died in 1910. The true quote is much older, and its original idea goes back as far as 1710 when writer Jonathan Swift, author of *Gulliver's Travels*, observed that "Falsehood flies, and the Truth comes limping after it," from which it has slowly developed (O'Toole, 2014). In any case, the sentiment is an astute one, and is almost prophetic in how applicable it is to the way social media are used, both to circulate and to consume inaccurate media. Indeed, in a rigorous study of how misinformation is transferred around on social media, Del Vicario et al (2016) found that:

Users tend to aggregate in communities of interest, which causes reinforcement and fosters confirmation bias, segregation, and polarization. This comes at the expense of the quality of the information and leads to proliferation of biased narratives fomented by unsubstantiated rumors, mistrust, and paranoia.

There is of course no denying that "filling the void" on social media platforms that are also increasingly used for access to news and informational media allows users to indulge readily in rumour, fantasy, conspiracy, defamation of character, and other patterns of misinformation, much faster and more efficiently than with any other form of media — ever. In Chapter Two, I referred to the popularity of hoax images and the appealing fantasies they contain as an example of how affect, even when triggered by a completely fictitious representation of the world, can have more value than verifiable information itself. The November 2015 case of Canadian journalist Veerender Jubbal is a good example of how widespread ignorance, of which digital misinformation is a primary symptom, can be harmful and dangerous, and is easily exacerbated in the ways that digital social networks are used to "fill the void." Jubbal, who is a Sikh, had shared a harmless selfie of himself in the reflection of his bathroom mirror, taken using the built-in camera of an iPad. After the attacks in Paris, which killed 130 people, members of the gaming community who were angry at Jubbal's characterisation of some computer games as racist, manipulated his mirror selfie was so that it showed him wearing what appeared to be a suicide vest and the iPad on which he was taking the image looked like some sort of book with an Islamic-looking binding, presumably a Qur'an. The gamers had also manipulated Jubbal's eyebrows to make him look more devious, and added a large, phallic sex toy in the background of the image, in a bid to use homosexuality to undermine both Jubbal and the pantomime-villain Islamic terrorist he became to those who didn't know him. The image was identified as a fake, but not before Italian TV news channel TG24 had tweeted the picture and conservative Spanish daily newspaper *La Razon* had put the image on its front page. There are a number of issues in this case that combined to terrible effect: the first is of course that social media enabled the spread of this image — cue widespread determinism. But the other factors in play here point to deeper societal issues. As a Sikh, Jubbal wears a turban in the image. While some Muslim men also wear turban-like headwear, these usually look quite different to Sikh turbans, yet nobody who shared the image was apparently interested or knowledgeable enough as to this difference to care. Another issue in this case was the desire of so many people to believe unquestioningly in Jubbal's image, particularly as a somewhat hirsute man of colour, as a portrayal of exactly the stereotypical terrorist that they had wanted to imagine. To produce such an image is abhorrent, but the actions of the gamers who did so revealed a far more widespread ignorance and racism.

Still images are one of the most potent formats via which misinformation can travel. As media sociologist Martin Hand reminds us, "At the level of theory, the advent of digital imaging is thought to have played a significant role in *destabilizing* these modern ways of seeing and knowing, radically questioning the objectivity or truth effect of the analogue photograph" (2012). When John Berger said "the relationship between what we see and what we know is never settled" (1990), he could not have foreseen quite how much the digital era would prove him right.

The image opposite is another good example of the kind of misleading visual content that is easily spread on social media, and which can cause real harm over time. It purports to expose the hypocrisy of environmentalists who have urged the use of electric and hybrid-electric vehicles. What the black-and-white representation of the image here cannot show is that the "lithium mine" at the top is a harsh shade of brown, while the "oilsands" site is idyllic and green by comparison. Far more troubling than the way the two images are placed next to each other to encourage the viewer's favour of the

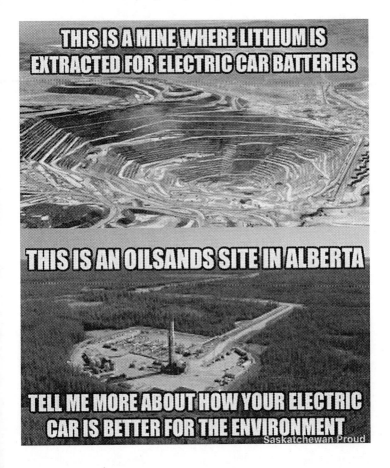

THIS IS A MINE WHERE LITHIUM IS EXTRACTED FOR ELECTRIC CAR BATTERIES

THIS IS AN OILSANDS SITE IN ALBERTA

TELL ME MORE ABOUT HOW YOUR ELECTRIC CAR IS BETTER FOR THE ENVIRONMENT

Saskatchewan Proud

lower image, however, is the fact that the item as a whole is completely inaccurate. According to blogger Mark Sumner (2016), the top image is in fact a copper mine, while the bottom, although related to tar sands oil extraction, is far from typical. Lithium is not mined at all — it is extracted from highly saline water, in harsh areas that already have little wildlife. Tar sands, on the other hand, have their oil extracted in an energy-intensive process very similar to mining that involves blasting and drilling, and which can require 42,475.27

litres (1,500 cubic feet) of natural gas to produce a single barrel of oil (Sumner, 2016).

The problem is not only that the image and its text have been deliberately fabricated to mislead, but that there is a clear cultural precedent for the existence and spread of such media, right down to the typeface — Impact Regular, usually uppercase, in white with a black outline. The familiar, idiomatic features of such media invite them to be categorised as a form of "folk" informational media, and can situate them subtly but unambiguously outside of mainstream media, encouraging those who have learned to distrust or ignore mainstream media to pay more attention. While experts may well be able to identify and debunk such images, the vast majority of people, who are viewing media in order to "fill the void," will neither attempt to do so, nor necessarily even imagine that the information they contain could be false.

Sometimes, rather than being deliberately misleading, untruths can spread online because they represent some sort of extreme, if believable, fantasy that is so outrageous, surprising, or upsetting that nobody bothers to check if it is true. A clear example of this can also be found in relation to the environment. In October 2016, an article appeared in *Outside Magazine* entitled "Obituary: Great Barrier Reef (25 Million BC–2016)." Its subtitle read "*Climate change and ocean acidification have killed off one of the most spectacular features on the planet.*" In addition to the horrific state of affairs implied by the headline — the Great Barrier Reef being a unique site of biodiversity and natural beauty — there was another problem: It was a wild exaggeration. After a recent "bleaching event," an occurrence in which corals expel algae and turn white, up to 22% of the corals in the Great Barrier Reef are thought to be dead. While this is obviously a tragedy, it is also misleading in a way that jeopardises the other 78% that remains alive. "The message should be that it isn't too late for Australia to lift its game and better protect the GBR, not [that] we should all give up because the GBR is supposedly dead," Terry

Hughes, director of the ARC Centre of Excellence for Coral Reef Studies, told the *Huffington Post* (2016). Here, while the story is based on a factual event, its hyperbole does far more harm than good. By overstating the case of how bad things are, it risked undermining the possibility that action might actually be taken.

Although in this case the item in question is an ordinary blog article, hosted outside of social networks, its rapid spread was still facilitated via social media. When highly salient media spread quickly, it is said that they have "gone viral." The capacity for media to "go viral" is greatly amplified by social media, which afford sharing with far greater ease. Features such as lists of content that is "trending" only enable further sharing, and Facebook has reportedly included false news stories in its "trending" section a number of times since automating the feature in 2016 (Dewey, 2016). The ability for rapid dissemination of content need neither be cast as an unqualified good or bad, but it is a hallmark of how social network platforms function, and cases such as those above show that it must be treated very cautiously. Karine Nahon and Jeff Hemsley (2013), who have greatly clarified and elucidated the concept of *virality* in its present usage, remind us that the origins of thinking about information according to this metaphor lie in the field of marketing. This provenance should come as no surprise, given that the social networks across which such "viral" flows of information occur are themselves so commercially orientated. It should also remind us that social media are never truly the beginning of the story.

Can we blame social media?

Events such as the British vote to leave the European Union, and especially the election of Donald Trump, resulted in a new wave of determinism in social media criticism. The logic appeared to be that these events were possible because of a "post-factual" relationship to media, against the backdrop of which there is "fake news" spreading on Facebook, and therefore that Facebook was largely responsible not only for the social divisions revealed by these issues, but for the lowest value in the Pound Sterling for thirty-one years and for President Trump. Technology journalist Olivia Solon wrote in the *Guardian* that "Rather than connecting people – as Facebook's euphoric mission statement claims – the bitter polarization of the social network over the last eighteen months suggests Facebook is actually doing more to divide the world" (2016). This should not be a convincing argument. If nothing else, it is largely a re-emergence of the same anxieties about user-generated content that had been heard from many of journalism's old guard after the advent of "web 2.0".

When it was put to Mark Zuckerberg that inaccurate media shared via Facebook might even have been a contributing factor in the election of Donald Trump, he responded that "the idea that fake news on Facebook… influenced the election…is a pretty crazy idea." At least in one important sense, Zuckerberg is not entirely wrong. Any sociologist familiar with the Rust Belt states (Hochschild, 2016), or the Leave-voting regions of England for that matter (Davies, 2016), will attest that there were and still are cultural, social and economic issues amongst the populations of these regions that had been brewing for years before the historic votes in 2016. To place the blame squarely on Facebook, even with all of the "fake news" that is distributed on it, is a determinist sticking-plaster solution that allows mainstream journalists to pat themselves on the back. Not only does it embrace the idea that conventional sources of news are never inaccurate or biased — an idea in which news audiences lost faith decades ago, it also allows the broader forces that drive "filling the void" to be left entirely unchallenged. If you wanted to find evidence for Facebook helping the Trump campaign, the fact that they were able to use Facebook's targeted ads to spread low-tech policy videos or produce a ten-fold increase in merchandising sales — providing much-needed campaign funding, would be a much safer hypothesis (Bertoni, 2016). Yet the unwavering belief in social media-powered digital misinformation as a direct causal factor persists. Computational social scientist Michela Del Vicario and colleagues tell us that "Digital misinformation has become so pervasive in online social media that it has been listed by the [World Economic Forum] as one of the main threats to human society" (2016). The fact that the World Economic Forum would be keen to blame technology should also be no surprise, and the WEF report to which Del Vicario and colleagues refer is an impressive work of superficial technologically-determinist pseudo-analysis that ignores entirely the interplay of culture and capital, worrying instead about how what it calls "digital wildfires" cause people to lose money.

The common antidote to technological determinism is to speak of what technology *allows*, rather than what it drives or causes, and we have seen above that social media do indeed *allow* some aspects of the post-factual era to be worse. While Facebook may be irresponsible, disinterested in the news, and exploitative of the "filling the void" pattern however, as a platform it is more of an enabler than a root cause. Social media's enabling role does need to be subjected to critique and exposure, and Mark Zuckerberg has even described some solutions to how these enabling effects may be ameliorated (2016), but we should be very clear that the affective potency of "fake news" and similar content, is part of the "filling the void" phenomenon described in this book, and is therefore primarily an aspect of the societies we live in, as opposed to the platforms we use. If we are to be critical of Facebook, we need to formulate better, more sophisticated arguments that can't be so easily deflected or batted away.

While Facebook and other social media are inescapably part of how information — and misinformation — spread through the public sphere, it isn't Facebook that might have skewed people's understanding of the issues, so much as the way people are already accustomed to using Facebook: For "filling the void", rather than learning in earnest about the world. Media and communications scholar Natalie Fenton has cogently observed of social media that "people rarely have democratic enhancement at the top of their agendas and use the internet far more for entertainment purposes than for informational gain" (2012). As media scholar Thomas E. Patterson (2010) says: "those who rhapsodize about the 'information age' ignore the human factor. Although public affairs information is more readily available than ever before, the key aspect, as it has always been, is the demand for it." If the affective experience of social media is akin to fried foods and stuffed-crust pizza, media that feature information itself, especially where they may be contradictory to pre-existing dispositions and opinions, are the equivalent of reminding people to eat their vegetables; they are the steaming plate of un-seasoned boiled spinach of the online media world.

If the emotional distress of late capitalism makes us so desperate for distraction, even if it is in the form of completely untrue news stories, is it not this state of affairs which we should be taking issue with? Journalists blaming Mark Zuckerberg for widespread misinformation before they blame Rupert Murdoch, as they did after Trump was elected, are simply trying not to bite the hand that feeds them. Of course there are things that Facebook and Twitter could do to mitigate the effects of how the spread of misinformation is enabled by their platforms, and the choice to lay off the human editors of their "trending" section and replace them with algorithmic functionality does not, in hindsight, look like a good move. However this move should remind us of Facebook's ruthless commerciality. There is a big difference between a simplistic "Facebook produces disinformation because it allows people to post misleading or heavily subjective content on there" and "Facebook's entire business is to exploit the emotional distress we experience as a result of the culture of late capitalism, by providing a stream of emotionally salient content." In the first argument, Facebook *is* the post-factual; in the second, it exploits it for commercial gain — hardly much better, but fundamentally different.

Recall from Chapter Four that Facebook's business model is to exploit our unhappiness and our desperation to "fill the void." Beyond issues of public perception, they have no incentive to change their platforms unless it helps them carry out their own business more effectively. Here, we return to the central themes of this book. Facebook, Twitter, and other social networks are no more interested in building a better public sphere or fighting the post-factual trend than they are in helping to fight social media addiction or improving privacy: Not at all. The rapid spread of highly affective yet inaccurate information is as important to Facebook's business model as "food porn" or selfies.

Afterword

What this book has hopefully illustrated is a pattern of human behaviour in relation to both late capitalism and the technologies it produces. In that sense, it isn't a book about social media at all, so much as the elements in us and in our capitalism that make social media possible. In the preface to this book I expressed the unfeasibility of broadly dictating how people should use online media, whether for the spread of information or for other purposes, and I reiterate that here. In any case, the solution to large and complex problems is rarely "more control." The answers, if they can be found, will not lie with social networks at all, but in the kind of society we have, and the kind of society we want. Mark Fisher (2009) has observed that:

> As any number of radical theorists from Brecht through to Foucault and Badiou have maintained, emancipatory politics must always destroy the appearance of a "natural order", must reveal what is presented as necessary and inevitable to be a mere contingency, just as it must make what was previously impossible seem attainable.

Despite the flippant "what social media is doing to us" newspaper columns and blog posts, part of this "natural order" has come to be the role of social networks in our lives — from providing us with distraction to making us dissatisfied with our bodies to enabling our access to inaccurate news-related media. What this book has tried to illustrate is that, rather than being unremarkable, the ways in which such platforms are used are highly problematic. As I have hopefully shown, this state of affairs is not inevitable, however. At every turn, we must problematise and draw attention to the ways that social media are exploiting our emotional distress for commercial gain, and challenge the enabling effects these media have for the worst behavioural aspects of our societies. Facts may have lost their "sacred" status, but facts are not necessarily needed for asking questions. The more we question not only the arrangement of interconnected features that comprise social media use that are detailed in this book, but the features of late-capitalist societies in general that make Facebook and other social media so appealing, the better chance there is of genuine, emancipatory change.

As stated at the outset, this is a book aimed at revealing important connections in order to explain and critique contemporary social media. Solutions to the problems highlighted are not a major feature of this work, but in order not to leave readers completely dangling, some ways to ameliorate the dysfunction of our relationship with social media platforms are explored briefly here.

Obviously, to the extent that your use of Facebook, Twitter, Instagram, or any other platform is detrimental to you, by far the best solution is the same as with any other exploitative and dysfunctional relationship: Leave. Close your Facebook, Twitter, LinkedIn, and Instagram accounts and the capacity for them to exploit you or cause you detriment is instantly curtailed. There is no such thing as a harmless, clean, unilateral use of social media; if you use them to any degree, they will use you too.

As acknowledged in Chapter One, however, it isn't that simple. One third of all Facebook users, numbering hundreds of millions of people and outnumbering the populations of most countries, have reportedly deactivated their account at some point, only to reactivate again (Baumer et al, 2013). We are not robots, we don't always take the most rational steps for our own wellbeing, and if our genuine social relations extend into a sphere into which we are completely impaired from venturing, this may at least feel more detrimental or impractical than the loss of time, sleep, and emotional wellbeing that are attributed to social media usage, never mind the merciless exploitation.

There are other ways that you can frustrate and reconfigure the terms of your relationship with social media platforms, depending on what you get from them, that may allow you to keep the benefits while being less useful to various groups of shareholders and Silicon Valley investors.

Limit the time you spend. Use a browser extension, or a service like Freedom, to limit how much time you are able to spend being distracted by social media websites. Five minutes, outside of working hours, and ten minutes at the weekend is enough. If you don't like the coercive aspect of browser plugins or other services that actually block your access to these sites, at least make a note of the time when you first start browsing on a social network, and the time when you stop. You can do this on your phone as well.

Prefer independent/ethical/decentralised alternatives. Particularly with messaging there are a range of alternatives, such as Signal. You don't have to use Facebook Messenger as a sole means for communication, and if you graciously invite your friends one-by-one to migrate their conversations with you and their other friends to these alternatives, the freedom will quickly spread. Likewise, although Google Search or Gmail are not social media, versions of the same advertising-driven data harvesting are in play, and your privacy is compromised by these policies, so use the independent, non-tracking DuckDuckGo for search and FastMail for email.

Limit the amount of data you give away. Post, like, retweet, and react seldom. All these actions are part of social networks largely so that you can give them valuable data about yourself and your friends. Click on ads even less. In fact, *never* click ads for things that genuinely interest you. Seriously never do this. Facebook makes about six billion dollars per quarter at the time of writing from mobile ad spending alone.

Corrupt the data. Why does your profile picture need to be you? Why does your gender need to be specified or be correctly specified? Why do you have to "like" the things you actually like? Start "liking" things you hate. Unlike pages you have previously liked (products especially, sources of posts may still be useful to you), like or follow things you don't like in reality, "join" events you have no intention of attending, and avoid RSVP-ing at all via social media where you do plan to attend, sending a message via another means instead. "Report" media that is not offensive; click on ads for things you are not interested in. You may even want to consider changing your name. Officially, Facebook has a "real names policy" and requires that you use your "real" identity, but in practice this policy is hard to enforce, and many people quietly continue to use false or incomplete names for a variety of reasons.

Put public pressure on social media platforms. They are very PR-conscious and have caved many times before when their attempts to exploit their users went too far. The truth is that they are constantly going too far in ways that all the same pass by unnoticed, and we should be calling them out far more than we do.

Build your own open technologies and support others to build ethical social media businesses. As discussed in Chapter One, there are lots of legitimate combinations for the web, media, and sociality. The most exciting and positive part of this overall picture is to imagine how the same technologies that have produced the patterns addressed in this book can be arranged and orchestrated in ways that celebrate culture, include everybody, and run with the grain of humanism. Social media are largely built on Free Software technologies like PHP and Ruby, which makes their unethical business models seem all the worse, and even when their founders did study computer science, such as Mark Zuckerberg, they often dropped out. Free Software is often both highly documented, meaning that self-teaching is an established pathway to their use, and low-cost. Even if you must build your own apps for closed platforms such as the App Store, you don't have to collect people's data — it's far better just to make useful tools for people and media experiences they can enjoy.

Delete the mobile apps and just use the websites. According to Facebook's quarterly results in July 2016, mobile ads bring in 84% of ad revenue. Even if you want to maintain some presence on social media sites for staying in touch with friends, deleting the apps can remove the temptation to use them excessively and prevent them from pervading your life.

Try not to care too much. Did you post something meaningful and get no likes or retweets? Be glad — that means Facebook and Twitter and their advertisers will pay less attention to the thing you posted. If the things you passionately care about are junk to your adversaries, that is a good thing. As for your friends, you know that they are on social media for affect; for arousal. Your post about a political opinion or news story may simply not be resonant enough along those dimensions, but that doesn't mean your friends or followers don't agree it's important — it's just that that sort of content may not be the reason why they're on Facebook or Twitter; it may not be what they're looking for.

Remember that your own "filling the void" on social media, while it may distract you from your sadness or depression in the short term, will make them worse almost immediately afterwards, and is ultimately the antithesis of everything that will make you happy. Such distractions do not provide time with your loved ones, enhance your creative pursuits, help you build a better world, support political self-determination, alleviate your work–life balance (since they are neither work nor life), educate you, bring you closer to your ambitions, or give your life meaning or purpose.

Reclaim "social media." We can and must learn lessons from what social media, in the normative sense, reveal about media consumption and use these to break through the post-factual sludge, whilst remaining committed to social justice. If the destruction of the "natural order" Fisher and others have identified can also be made entertaining, affective, and even hedonic, then all media makers, from musicians to journalists to university academics publishing research, can reclaim the idea of "social media" by producing media and culture that use these hallmarks to undermine the artificial, cruel stability of late capitalism and build something better. If there is a role for media to play in an increasingly unstable world, not just in a journalistic sense but in the broadest sense of the word "media," it can and should be the radical questioning of social media's seeming inevitability and normalisation. In doing so, we can also claim that which doesn't feature in the timeline at all: The future.

Bibliography

Abunimah, A. (2015) *Israeli lawmaker's call for genocide of Palestinians gets thousands of Facebook likes.* Available at: https://electronicintifada.net/blogs/ali-abunimah/israeli-lawmakers-call-genocide-palestinians-gets-thousands-facebook-likes (Accessed: September 2016).

Adam, T.C. and Epel, E.S. (2007) 'Stress, eating and the reward system', *Physiology & Behavior*, 91(4), pp. 449–458. doi: 10.1016/j.physbeh.2007.04.011.

Alvesson, M. (2013) *The triumph of emptiness: Consumption, higher education, and work organization.* Oxford: Oxford University Press.

Anderson, C. (2009) *Free: The Future of a Radical Price.* New York: Hyperion.

Angwin, J. and Parris, T. (2016) *Facebook lets advertisers exclude users by race.* Available at: https://www.propublica.org/article/facebook-lets-advertisers-exclude-users-by-race (Accessed: October 2016).

Arendt, H. (1951) *The Origins of Totalitarianism.* Schocken Books.

Arnetz, B.B., Akerstedt, T., Hillert, L., Lowden, A., Kuster, N. and Wiholm, C. (2008) 'The effects of 884 MHz GSM wireless communication signals on self-reported symptom and sleep (EEG)- an experimental provocation study', *PIERS Online*, 3(7), pp. 1148–1150. doi: 10.2529/piers060907172142.

Balkan, A. (2015) *Beyond the Camera Panopticon.* Available at: https://re-publica.com/session/beyond-camera-panopticon (Accessed: 30 May 2016).

Barlow, J.P. (2016) *A Declaration of the Independence of Cyberspace.* Available at: https://www.eff.org/cyberspace-independence (Accessed: 1 October 2010).

Bauman, Z. (2001) 'Consuming life', *Journal of Consumer Culture*, 1(1), pp. 9–29. doi: 10.1177/146954050100100102.

—— (2007) *Consuming life.* Cambridge: Polity Press.

Baumer, E.P.S., Adams, P., Khovanskaya, V.D., Liao, T.C., Smith, M.E., Schwanda Sosik, V. and Williams, K. (2013) 'Limiting, leaving, and (re)lapsing: an exploration of Facebook non-use practices and experiences', *Proceedings of the SIGCHI Conference on Human Factors in Computing Systems - CHI '13*. doi: 10.1145/ 2470654.2466446.

BBC (2010) *S Korea child 'starves as parents raise virtual baby'*. Available at: http://news.bbc.co.uk/2/hi/8551122.stm (Accessed: 2 August 2016).

Bell, E. (2016) *Facebook is eating the world*. Available at: http://www.cjr.org/analysis/facebook_and_media.php (Accessed: 8 March 2016).

Berger, J. (1990) *'Ways of Seeing': Based on the BBC television series*. London, Eng.: British Broadcasting Corp.

Bertoni, S. (2016) *Exclusive interview: How Jared Kushner won trump the white house*. Available at: http://www.forbes.com/sites/stevenbertoni/2016/11/22/exclusive-interview-how-jared-kushner-won-trump-the-white-house/ (Accessed: November 2016).

Bingham, J. (2016) *How teenage pregnancy collapsed after birth of social media*. Available at: http://www.telegraph.co.uk/news/health/news/12189376/How-teenage-pregnancy-collapsed-after-birth-of-socialmedia.html (Accessed: March 2016).

Black, E. (2012) *IBM and the holocaust: The strategic alliance between Nazi Germany and America's most powerful corporation*. 3rd edn. Washington, D.C.: Dialog Press.

Bown, A. (2015) *Enjoying It: Candy Crush and Capitalism*. United Kingdom: Zero Books.

boyd, danah m. and Ellison, N.B. (2007) 'Social network sites: Definition, history, and scholarship', *Journal of Computer-Mediated Communication*, 13(1), pp. 210–230. doi: 10.1111/j.1083-6101.2007.00393.x.

Brown, W. (2015) *Undoing the Demos: Neoliberalism's Stealth Revolution*. United States: Zone Books.

BuzzFeed (2014) *How technology is changing media*. Available at: http://insights.buzzfeed.com/industry-trends-2014/ (Accessed: 10 September 2016).

Cacioppo, J.T. and Patrick, W. (2009) *Loneliness: Human Nature and the Need for Social Connection*. New York: W. W. Norton & Company.

Cadwalladr, C. (2013) *My week as an Amazon insider*. Available at: https://www.theguardian.com/technology/2013/dec/01/week-amazon-insider-feature-treatment-employees-work (Accessed: September 2016).

——. (2016) *View from wales: Town showered with EU cash votes to leave EU*. Available at: https://www.theguardian.com/uk-news/2016/jun/25/view-wales-town-showered-eu-cash-votes-leave-ebbw-vale (Accessed: July 2016).

Campbell, D. and Siddique, H. (2016) *Mental illness soars among young women in England – survey*. Available at: https://www.theguardian.com/

lifeandstyle/2016/sep/29/self-harm-ptsd-and-mental-illness-soaring-among-young-women-in-england-survey (Accessed: September 2016).

Carr, A. (2016) *I found out my secret internal tinder rating and now I wish I hadn't*. Available at: http://www.fastcompany.com/3054871/whats-your-tinder-score-inside-the-apps-internal-ranking-system (Accessed: 29 June 2016).

Carr, N. (2010) *The Shallows: What the Internet is Doing to Our Brains*. New York: W. W. Norton & Company.

Chakrabortty, A. and Weale, S. (2016) *Universities accused of 'importing sports direct model' for lecturers' pay*. Available at: https://www.theguardian.com/uk-news/2016/nov/16/universities-accused-of-importing-sports-direct-model-for-lecturers-pay (Accessed: November 2016).

Chang, S., Stuckler, D., Yip, P. and Gunnell, D. (2013) 'Impact of 2008 global economic crisis on suicide: Time trend study in 54 countries', *BMJ*, 347(sep17 1), pp. f5239. doi: 10.1136/bmj.f5239.

Childress, C.C. (2012) 'All media are social', *Contexts*, 11(1), pp. 55–57. doi: 10.1177/1536504212436499.

Chou, H.-T.G. and Edge, N. (2012) '"They are happier and having better lives than I Am": The impact of using Facebook on perceptions of others' lives', *Cyberpsychology, Behavior, and Social Networking*, 15(2), pp. 117–121. doi: 10.1089/cyber.2011.0324.

Christie, J. (2015) *Mom 'was Facebook chatting behind the wheel during fatal horror crash'*. Available at: http://www.dailymail.co.uk/news/article-2980374/Mom-Facebook-chatting-wheel-horror-crash-killed-daughter-11-two-young-nieces-police-say.html (Accessed: 25 July 2016).

Conan (2013) TBS, 20 September.

Coccurello, R., D'Amato, F.R. and Moles, A. (2009) 'Chronic social stress, hedonism and vulnerability to obesity: Lessons from rodents', *Neuroscience & Biobehavioral Reviews*, 33(4), pp. 537–550. doi: 10.1016/j.neubiorev.2008.05.018.

Cohen, J.E. (2007) 'Cyberspace as/and space', *Columbia Law Review*, 107(1), pp. 210–256. doi: 10.2307/40041711.

Colapinto, J. (2007) *The Interpreter - Has a remote Amazonian tribe upended our understanding of language?* Available at: http://www.newyorker.com/magazine/2007/04/16/the-interpreter-2 (Accessed: 20 April 2015).

Coley, R. and Lockwood, D. (2012) *Cloud Time: The Inception of the Future*. United Kingdom: Zero Books.

Cosgrove, L., Krimsky, S., Vijayaraghavan, M. and Schneider, L. (2006) 'Financial ties between DSM-IV panel members and the pharmaceutical industry', *Psychotherapy and Psychosomatics*, 75(3), pp. 154–160. doi: 10.1159/000091772.

Crary, J. (2014) *24/7: Late Capitalism and the Ends of Sleep.* United Kingdom: Verso Books.

Curran, J., Fenton, N. and Freedman, D. (2012) *Misunderstanding the Internet.* New York: Taylor & Francis.

Curtis, A., (2016) *HyperNormalisation.* BBC iPlayer.

Davidson, R.J. (2003) 'Seven sins in the study of emotion: Correctives from affective neuroscience', *Brain and Cognition*, 52(1), pp. 129–132. doi: 10.1016/s0278-2626(03)00015-0.

Davies, J. (2011) *The importance of Suffering: The Value and Meaning of Emotional Discontent.* London: Taylor & Francis.

Davies, W. (2016) *The sociology of Brexit.* Available at: https://www. thesociologicalreview.com/blog/the-sociology-of-brexit.html (Accessed: October 2016).

Deger, A. (2016) *Israel jails Palestinian beautician over Facebook post.* Available at: http://www.aljazeera.com/news/2016/05/israel-jails-palestinian-beaut ician-facebook-post-160509132438229.html (Accessed: October 2016).

Del Vicario, M., Bessi, A., Zollo, F., Petroni, F., Scala, A., Caldarelli, G., Stanley, H.E. and Quattrociocchi, W. (2016) 'The spreading of misinformation online', *Proceedings of the National Academy of Sciences*, 113(3), pp. 554–559. doi: 10.1073/pnas.1517441113.

Deuze, M. (2005) 'What is journalism? Professional identity and ideology of journalists reconsidered', *Journalism*, 6(4), pp. 442–464. doi: 10.1177/1464884905056815.

Dewey, C. (2016) *Facebook has repeatedly trended fake news since firing its human editors.* Available at: https://www.washingtonpost.com/news/the-intersect/wp/2016/10/12/facebook-has-repeatedly-trended-fake-news-since-firing-its-human-editors/ (Accessed: October 2016).

Dodds, L. (2015) *Mapped: Where is Ukip's support strongest? Where there are no immigrants.* Available at: http://www.telegraph.co.uk/news/politics/ukip/11539388/Mapped-where-is-Ukips-support-strongest-Where-there-are-no-immigrants.html (Accessed: June 2016).

Doré, L. (2016a) *British people happy to be poorer if it means fewer foreigners, poll shows.* Available at: https://www.indy100.com/article/brexit-immigration-negotiations-relocating-banks-trade-migrants-economy-latest-7381081 (Accessed: October 2016).

——. (2016b) *The list.* Available at: http://indy100.independent.co.uk/article/daily-express-highlights-benefits-of-brexit-is-forced-to-retract-entire-article--bygEsaSHY8b (Accessed: 30 July 2016).

Drapeau, V., Therrien, F., Richard, D. and Tremblay, A. (2003) 'Is visceral obesity a physiological adaptation to stress?', *Panminerva medica*, 45(3), pp. 189–195.

Drugs.com (2000) *Citalopram (Celexa) uses, dosage, side effects*. Available at: https://www.drugs.com/citalopram.html (Accessed: September 2016).

Dunbar, R.I.M. (2016) 'Do online social media cut through the constraints that limit the size of offline social networks?', *Royal Society Open Science*, 3(1), p. 150292. doi: 10.1098/rsos.150292.

Dunn, J. (2015) *Youngsters won't join navy because they can't go on Facebook*. Available at: http://www.dailymail.co.uk/news/article-3207736/Young sters-don-t-want-serve-Royal-Navy-submarines-t-log-Facebook-waves. html (Accessed: October 2015).

Edge, A. (2015) *The ethics of autoplay video on Facebook: To play or not to play?* Available at: https://www.themediabriefing.com/article/the-ethics-of-autoplay-video-on-facebook-to-play-or-not-to-play (Accessed: August 2016).

Etehad, M. (2014) *OPINION: The dangerous influence of online hate speech in Gaza*. Available at: http://america.aljazeera.com/opinions/2014/7/gaza-israel-palestiniantwitterfacebook.html (Accessed: August 2016).

Facebook (2016) *News feed FYI: Further reducing Clickbait in feed | Facebook newsroom*. Available at: http://newsroom.fb.com/news/2016/08/news-feed-fyi-further-reducing-clickbait-in-feed/ (Accessed: 5 August 2016).

Fffffat (2014) *5-Star graffiti*. Available at: http://fffff.at/5-star-graffiti/ (Accessed: October 2016).

Fisher, M. (2009) *Capitalist Realism: Is there no Alternative?* United Kingdom: Zero Books.

Foster, D. (2016) *Lean Out*. United Kingdom: Repeater Books.

Fromm, E. (2001) *The Sane Society (Routledge classics)*. 2nd edn. London: Routledge.

Fung, B. (2016) *The British are frantically Googling what the E.U. Is, hours after voting to leave it*. Available at: https://www.washingtonpost.com/news/the-switch/wp/2016/06/24/the-british-are-frantically-googling-what-the-eu-is-hours-after-voting-to-leave-it/ (Accessed: 25 June 2016).

Galbraith, J.K. (1999) *The Affluent Society*. London: Penguin Books.

Gallup, Inc. (2013) *TV is Americans' main source of news*. Available at: http://www.gallup.com/poll/163412/americans-main-source-news.aspx (Accessed: October 2016).

Garcia, D., Kappas, A., Küster, D. and Schweitzer, F. (2016) 'The dynamics of emotions in online interaction', *Royal Society Open Science*, 3(8), p. 160059. doi: 10.1098/rsos.160059.

Garun, N. (2016) *Facebook says Philando Castile shooting video was temporarily removed due to a 'technical glitch'*. Available at: http://thenextweb.com/facebook/2016/07/07/yeah-ok/ (Accessed: July 2016).

Gilroy-Ware, M. (2013) 'Is Social Media Making Us Lonely', *Tech City News* (November), pp. 37–38.

Gitelman, L. and Pingree, G.B. (eds.) (2003) *New Media, 1740-1915.* Cambridge, MA: MIT Press.

Gitlin, T. (2003) *Media Unlimited: How the Torrent of Images and Sounds Overwhelms our Lives.* New York: Owl Books, U.S.

Goldrick-Rab, S., Kelchen, R., Harris, D.N. and Benson, J. (2016) 'Reducing income inequality in educational attainment: Experimental evidence on the impact of financial aid on college completion', *American Journal of Sociology*, 121(6), pp. 1762–1817. doi: 10.1086/685442.

Goodley, S. and Ashby, J. (2015) *Revealed: How sports direct effectively pays below minimum wage.* Available at: https://www.theguardian.com/business/2015/dec/09/how-sports-direct-effectively-pays-below-minimum-wage-pay (Accessed: September 2016).

Gosline, A. (2007) *Bored to death: Chronically bored people exhibit higher risk-taking behavior.* Available at: https://www.scientificamerican.com/article/the-science-of-boredom/ (Accessed: 25 September 2016).

Gottfried, J. and Shearer, E. (2016) *News use across social media platforms 2016.* Available at: http://www.journalism.org/2016/05/26/news-use-across-social-media-platforms-2016/ (Accessed: June 2016).

Greenfield, D.N. (1999) *Virtual Addiction: Help for Netheads, Cyber Freaks, and Those who Love Them.* Oakland, CA: New Harbinger Publications.

Greenwald, G. (2016) *Facebook is collaborating with the Israeli government to determine what should be censored.* Available at: https://theintercept.com/2016/09/12/facebook-is-collaborating-with-the-israeli-government-to-determine-what-should-be-censored/ (Accessed: 13 September 2016).

Gross, J.J. (1998) 'The emerging field of emotion regulation: An integrative review', *Review of General Psychology*, 2(3), pp. 271–299. doi: 10.1037/1089-2680.2.3.271.

Guardian (2014) *40% of managers avoid hiring younger women to get around maternity leave.* Available at: https://www.theguardian.com/money/2014/aug/12/managers-avoid-hiring-younger-women-maternity-leave (Accessed: 7 October 2016).

Hand, M. (2012) *Ubiquitous Photography.* Cambridge: John Wiley & Sons.

Hardt, M. and Negri, A. (2001) *Empire.* 10th edn. Cambridge, MA: Harvard University Press.

Hawton, K. and Haw, C. (2013) 'Economic recession and suicide', *BMJ*, 347(sep17 1), pp. f5612. doi: 10.1136/bmj.f5612.

Herman, E.S. and Chomsky, N. (1988) *Manufacturing Consent: The Political Economy of the Mass Media.* New York: Knopf Doubleday Publishing Group.

Hershkovits, D. (2015) *John Perry Barlow talks acid, Cyber-Independence and his friendship with JFK Jr.* Available at: http://www.papermag.com/

john-perry-barlow-talks-acid-cyber-independence-and-his-friendship-wit-1427554020.html (Accessed: 9 September 2016).

Hertwig, R. and Engel, C. (2016) 'Homo Ignorans: Deliberately choosing not to know', *Perspectives on Psychological Science*, 11(3), pp. 359–372. doi: 10.1177/1745691616635594.

Hochschild, A.R. (1979) 'Emotion work, feeling rules, and social structure', *American Journal of Sociology*, 85(3), pp. 551–575. doi: 10.2307/2778583.

——. (1997) 'When Work Becomes Home And Home Becomes Work', *California Management Review*, 39(4), pp. 79–97.

——. (2016) *Strangers in their own land: Anger and mourning on the American right*. United States: The New Press.

Hodgkinson, T. (2008) *With friends like these*. Available at: https://www.theguardian.com/technology/2008/jan/14/facebook (Accessed: 1 July 2015).

Hofmann, W., Kotabe, H. and Luhmann, M. (2013) 'The spoiled pleasure of giving in to temptation', *Motivation and Emotion*, 37(4), pp. 733–742. doi: 10.1007/s11031-013-9355-4.

Hofmann, W., Vohs, K.D. and Baumeister, R.F. (2012) 'What people desire, feel conflicted about, and try to resist in everyday life', *Psychological Science*, 23(6), pp. 582–588. doi: 10.1177/0956797612437426.

Holzman, D.C. (2010) 'What's in a color? The unique human health effects of blue light', *Environmental Health Perspectives*, 118(1), pp. A22–A27. doi: 10.1289/ehp.118-a22.

Honan, M. (2012) *Google's broken promise: The end of 'don't be evil'*. Available at: http://gizmodo.com/5878987/its-official-google-is-evil-now (Accessed: 20 May 2016).

Hough, A. (2011) *Student 'addiction' to technology 'similar to drug cravings', study finds*. Available at: http://www.telegraph.co.uk/technology/news/8436831/Student-addiction-to-technology-similar-to-drug-cravings-study-finds.html (Accessed: 24 January 2016).

Isaac, M. and Ember, S. (2016) *Facebook to change news feed to focus on friends and family*. Available at: http://www.nytimes.com/2016/06/30/technology/facebook-to-change-news-feed-to-focus-on-friends-and-family.html (Accessed: 28 August 2016).

James, O. (2008) *The Selfish Capitalist: Origins of Affluenza*. London: Vermilion.

——. (2010) *Britain on the Couch: Why We're Unhappier Compared with 1950, Despite Being Richer – A Treatment for the Low-Serotonin Society*. 2nd edn. London: Arrow Books.

Jeong, S. (2016) *How panics about pictures of naked women shaped the web as we know it*. Available at: https://www.washingtonpost.com/posteverything/wp/2016/08/19/how-panics-about-naked-pictures-of-women-shaped-the-web-as-we-know-it/ (Accessed: 21 August 2016).

Kane, A. (2016) *Israel targeting Palestinian protesters on Facebook*. Available at: https://theintercept.com/2016/07/07/israel-targeting-palestinian-protesters-on-facebook/ (Accessed: July 2016).

Kassel, J.D. (2000) 'Smoking and stress: Correlation, causation, and context', *American Psychologist*, 55(10), pp. 1155–1156. doi: 10.1037/0003-066x.55.10.1155.

Keen, A. (2008) *The Cult of the Amateur: How blogs, MySpace, YouTube, and the rest of today's user-generated media are destroying our economy, our culture, and our values*. New York: Crown Publishing Group.

Kelly, H. (2016) *Apple replaces the pistol emoji with a water gun*. Available at: http://money.cnn.com/2016/08/01/technology/apple-pistol-emoji/index.html (Accessed: 2 August 2016).

Khalid, A. (2016) *The emoji that unlocks hidden porn on Instagram*. Available at: http://www.dailydot.com/irl/how-to-find-porn-on-instagram/ (Accessed: 12 September 2016).

Kirkpatrick, D. (2010) *The Facebook Effect: The Inside Story of the Company that is Connecting the World*. New York: Simon & Schuster Adult Publishing Group.

Knapton, S. (2016) *Facebook users have 155 friends - but would trust just four in a crisis*. Available at: http://www.telegraph.co.uk/news/science/science-news/12108412/Facebook-users-have-155-friends-but-would-trust-just-four-in-a-crisis.html (Accessed: 22 September 2016).

Knowles, K. (2016a) *Emo smart homes know to pop the kettle on when you're sad*. Available at: http://www.thememo.com/2016/10/12/smart-homes-internet-of-things-iot-eq-radio-mit-technology-science/ (Accessed: 25 October 2016).

——. (2016b) *VR Porn: This virtual porn site lets you have sex with real women*. Available at: http://www.thememo.com/2016/07/26/vr-porn-cam-soda-vr-porn-kiiroo-sex-toys-cam-soda-virtual-reality-porn/ (Accessed: 26 July 2016).

Kramer, A.D.I., Guillory, J.E. and Hancock, J.T. (2014) 'Experimental evidence of massive-scale emotional contagion through social networks', *Proceedings of the National Academy of Sciences*, 111(24), pp. 8788–8790. doi: 10.1073/pnas.1320040111.

Kross, E., Verduyn, P., Demiralp, E., Park, J., Lee, D.S., Lin, N., Shablack, H., Jonides, J. and Ybarra, O. (2013) 'Facebook use predicts declines in subjective well-being in young adults', *PLoS ONE*, 8(8), p. e69841. doi: 10.1371/journal.pone.0069841.

Lair, D.J., Sullivan, K. and Cheney, G. (2005) 'Marketization and the Recasting of the professional self: The rhetoric and ethics of personal Branding', *Management Communication Quarterly*, 18(3), pp. 307–343. doi: 10.1177/0893318904270744.

Lee, A. (2011) *Photo sharing sites can sell your images if they want*. Available at: http://www.huffingtonpost.com/2011/05/11/twitpic-copyright_n_860 554.html (Accessed: 28 September 2016).

Levi, P. (1974) 'A Past We Thought Would Never Return', *Corriere della Sera*, 8 May.

Lewandowsky, S., Ecker, U.K.H., Seifert, C.M., Schwarz, N. and Cook, J. (2012) 'Misinformation and its correction: Continued influence and successful Debiasing', *Psychological Science in the Public Interest*, 13(3), pp. 106–131. doi: 10.1177/1529100612451018.

Lin, L. yi, Sidani, J.E., Shensa, A., Radovic, A., Miller, E., Colditz, J.B., Hoffman, B.L., Giles, L.M. and Primack, B.A. (2016) 'Association Between Social Media Use and Depression Among U.S. Young Adults', *Depression and Anxiety*, 33(4), pp. 323–331. doi: 10.1002/da.22466.

Linebaugh, P. (2009) *The Magna Carta Manifesto: Liberties and Commons for All*. Berkeley, CA: University of California Press.

Looft, C. (2015) *The WorldStar of war Porn*. Available at: http://motherboard. vice.com/read/the-worldstar-of-war-porn (Accessed: 25 July 2016).

Lovink, G. (2012) *Networks Without a Cause: A Critique of Social Media*. Cambridge, UK: John Wiley & Sons.

Lup, K., Trub, L. and Rosenthal, L. (2015) 'Instagram #Instasad? Exploring associations among Instagram use, Depressive symptoms, negative social comparison, and strangers followed', *Cyberpsychology, Behavior, and Social Networking*, 18(5), pp. 247–252. doi: 10.1089/cyber.2014.0560.

MacKinnon, C.A. and Dworkin, A. (1988) *Pornography and Civil Rights: A New Day for Women's Equality*. Minneapolis: Organizing Against Pornography.

MacKinnon, R. (2012) *Consent of the Networked: The World-Wide Struggle for Internet Freedom*. New York: The Perseus Books Group.

Manovich, L. (2002) *The Language of New Media*. 8th edn. Cambridge, MA: MIT Press.

Martinez, D., Orlowska, D., Narendran, R., Slifstein, M., Liu, F., Kumar, D., Broft, A., Van Heertum, R. and Kleber, H.D. (2010) 'Dopamine type 2/3 receptor availability in the Striatum and social status in human volunteers', *Biological Psychiatry*, 67(3), pp. 275–278. doi: 10.1016/j. biopsych.2009.07.037.

May, A. (2016) *Man using wanted poster as Facebook profile picture arrested*. Available at: http://www.usatoday.com/story/news/nation-now/2016/09/07/man-using-wanted-poster-facebook-profile-picture-arrested/89949172/ (Accessed: September 2016).

Mayer-Schönberger, V. (2011) *Delete: The Virtue of Forgetting in the Digital Age*. 4th edn. United States: Princeton University Press.

McKenzie, S. (2016) *The #HijackSelfie that wasn't a selfie*. Available at: http://
edition.cnn.com/2016/03/30/europe/egyptair-hijacked-plane-selfie/
index.html (Accessed: July 2016).

McRobbie, A. (2015) *Is passionate work a neoliberal delusion?* Available at:
https://www.opendemocracy.net/transformation/angela-mcrobbie/
is-passionate-work-neoliberal-delusion (Accessed: April 2015).

Mc Mahon, C. (2015) *Why do we 'like' social media?* Available at: https://
thepsychologist.bps.org.uk/volume-28/september-2015/why-do-we-
social-media (Accessed: January 2016).

Meier, A., Reinecke, L. and Meltzer, C.E. (2016) '"Facebocrastination"?
Predictors of using Facebook for procrastination and its effects on
students' well-being', *Computers in Human Behavior*, 64, pp. 65–76. doi:
10.1016/j.chb.2016.06.011.

Meier, E.P. and Gray, J. (2014) 'Facebook photo activity associated with body
image disturbance in adolescent girls', *Cyberpsychology, Behavior, and
Social Networking*, 17(4), pp. 199–206. doi: 10.1089/cyber.2013.0305.

Meikle, J. (2016) *Antidepressant prescriptions in England double in a
decade*. Available at: https://www.theguardian.com/society/2016/jul/05/
antidepressant-prescriptions-in-england-double-in-a-decade (Accessed:
September 2016).

Meyer, E. (2014) *Inadvertent Algorithmic cruelty*. Available at: http://
meyerweb.com/eric/thoughts/2014/12/24/inadvertent-algorithmic-
cruelty/ (Accessed: December 2014).

Miller, D., Costa, E., Haynes, N., McDonald, T., Nicolescu, R., Sinanan, J.,
Spyer, J., Venkatraman, S. and Wang, X. (2016) *How the world changed
social media*. United Kingdom: UCL Press.

Moeller, S., Powers, E. and Roberts, J. (2012) '"El mundo desconectado"
y "24 horas sin medios": Alfabetización mediática para la conciencia
crítica de los jóvenes', *Comunicar: Revista Científica de Comunicación y
Educación*, 20(39), pp. 45–52. doi: 10.3916/c39-2012-02-04.http://www.
revistacomunicar.com/indice-en/articulo.php?numero=39-2012-06

Monbiot, G. (2016a) *Neoliberalism is creating loneliness. That's what's
wrenching society apart*. Available at: https://www.theguardian.com/
commentisfree/2016/oct/12/neoliberalism-creating-loneliness-
wrenching-society-apart (Accessed: 15 October 2016).

——. (2016b) *Neoliberalism – the ideology at the root of all our problems*.
Available at: https://www.theguardian.com/books/2016/apr/15/neoliber
alism-ideology-problem-george-monbiot (Accessed: 23 April 2016).

Morozov, E.V. (2011) *The net delusion: The dark side of Internet freedom*. New
York, NY: Allen Lane.

Muise, A., Christofides, E. and Desmarais, S. (2009) 'More information than
you ever wanted: Does Facebook bring out the green-eyed monster of

jealousy?', *CyberPsychology & Behavior*, 12(4), pp. 441–444. doi: 10.1089/cpb.2008.0263.

Myrick, J.G. (2015) 'Emotion regulation, procrastination, and watching cat videos online: Who watches Internet cats, why, and to what effect?', *Computers in Human Behavior*, 52, pp. 168–176. doi: 10.1016/j.chb.2015.06.001.

Nadkarni, A. and Hofmann, S.G. (2012) 'Why do people use Facebook?', *Personality and Individual Differences*, 52(3), pp. 243–249. doi: 10.1016/j.paid.2011.11.007.

Nahon, K. and Hemsley, J. (2013) *Going Viral*. Cambridge: Polity Press.

O'Carroll, L. and Jones, S. (2016) *'It was a fake meeting': Byron Hamburgers staff on immigration raid*. Available at: https://www.theguardian.com/uk-news/2016/jul/28/it-was-a-fake-meeting-byron-hamburgers-staff-on-immigration-raid (Accessed: August 2016).

O'Connell, S. (2005) *Sugar: The Grass that Changed the World*. London: Virgin Books.

O'Leary, J. (2016) *Do EU immigrants contribute £1.34 for every £1 received from the UK?* Available at: https://fullfact.org/immigration/do-eu-immigrants-contribute-134-every-1-they-receive/ (Accessed: March 2016).

O'Toole, G. (2014) *Quote investigator*. Available at: http://quote investigator.com/2014/07/13/truth/ (Accessed: October 2016).

Patterson, T.E. (2010) 'Media abundance and democracy', *Revista media & jornalismo*, 9(2), pp. 13–29. <http://cimj.org/images/stories/docs_cimj/17-1-artigo.pdf>

Patton, J.H. (2014) 'Sensation Seeking', in *Encyclopedia of human behavior*. Edited by Vilanayur S Ramachandran. 2nd edn. United States: Elsevier Science.

Penney, J. (2016) 'Chilling effects: Online surveillance and Wikipedia use by Jon Penney: SSRN', *Berkeley Technology Law Journal*, 31(1), pp. 117–182.

Phillips, P. (2004) *Censored: The Top 25 Censored Stories: 2005*. New York: Seven Stories Press.

Power, N. (2009) *One dimensional woman*. United Kingdom: Zero Books.

Press Gazette (2015) *NRS: Daily mail most popular UK newspaper in print and online with 23m readers a month*. Available at: http://www.pressgazette.co.uk/nrs-daily-mail-most-popular-uk-newspaper-print-and-online-23m-readers-month/ (Accessed: October 2016).

Prior, M. (2007) *Post-Broadcast Democracy: How Media Choice Increases Inequality in Political Involvement and Polarizes Elections*. Cambridge: Cambridge University Press.

Proctor, R. and Schiebinger, L. (eds.) (2008) *Agnotology: The Making and Unmaking of Ignorance*. United States: Stanford University Press.

Protalinski, E. (2014) *Android and iOS users spend 32% of their App time playing games.* Available at: http://thenextweb.com/mobile/ 2014/04/01/ flurry-android-ios-users-spend-32-app-time-playing-games-17-facebook-14-browser/ (Accessed: September 2015).

Rae, J.R. and Lonborg, S.D. (2015) 'Do motivations for using Facebook moderate the association between Facebook use and psychological well-being?', *Frontiers in Psychology*, 6. doi: 10.3389/fpsyg.2015.00771.

Reeves, B. and Nass, C. (1998) *The Media Equation: How People Treat Computers, Television, and New Media like Real People and Places.* United States: Center for the Study of Language and Inf.

Roberts, J.A., Pullig, C. and Manolis, C. (2015) 'I need my smartphone: A hierarchical model of personality and cell-phone addiction', *Personality and Individual Differences*, 79, pp. 13–19. doi: 10.1016/j.paid.2015.01.049.

Roberts, R. (2015) *Psychology and Capitalism: The Manipulation of Mind.* United Kingdom: Zero Books.

Rosling, H. (2007) *The best stats you've ever seen.* Available at: https://youtu.be/hVimVzgtD6w.

Rudolph, C. (2016) *Apple finally releases rainbow flag Emoji.* Available at: http://www.newnownext.com/rainbow-flag-emoji-apple/08/2016/ (Accessed: August 2016).

Rushkoff, D. (2016) *Throwing Rocks at the Google Bus: How Growth became the Enemy of Prosperity.* United Kingdom: Portfolio Penguin.

Rushton, K. (2013) *Murdoch sale led to ruin of MySpace, says its co-founder.* Available at: http://www.telegraph.co.uk/finance/newsbysector/media technologyandtelecoms/digital-media/10455975/Murdoch-sale-led-to-ruin-of-MySpace-says-its-co-founder.html (Accessed: October 2016).

Samuelson, K. (2016) *Bride marries her literary Twitter crush after asking him out.* Available at: http://www.dailymail.co.uk/femail/article-3695711/ Bride-developed-crush-stranger-Waterstones-Twitter-feed-MARRIES-three-years-later.html (Accessed: July 2016).

Scally, D. (2016) *Austrian teen sues parents over embarrassing Facebook photos.* Available at: http://www.irishtimes.com/news/world/europe/austrian-teen-sues-parents-over-embarrassing-facebook-photos-1.2791353 (Accessed: 16 September 2016).

Schwartz, B. (2005) *The Paradox of Choice: Why More is Less.* New York: HarperCollins Publishers.

Smiley, L. (2015) *The shut-in economy – matter.* Available at: https://medium.com/matter/the-shut-in-economy-ec3ec1294816 (Accessed: 28 March 2015).

Smith, E. (2016) *Why we need to remember how to forget.* Available at: https://theconversation.com/why-we-need-to-remember-how-to-forget-53526 (Accessed: March 2016).

Smith IV, J. (2015) *Facebook is tracking your likes and selling them to advertisers.* Available at: https://mic.com/articles/125474/facebook-is-tracking-your-likes-and-selling-them-to-advertisers (Accessed: September 2016).

Smith, O. (2016) *The big bedroom invasion: Smartphones scuppering your sleep and sex.* Available at: http://www.thememo.com/2016/09/26/smartphones-smartphone-deloitte-paul-lee-sleep-the-big-bedroom-invasion-are-smartphones-scuppering-your-sleep-and-sex/ (Accessed: September 2016).

Solon, O. (2016) *Facebook's failure: Did fake news and polarized politics get trump elected?* Available at: https://www.theguardian.com/technology/2016/nov/10/facebook-fake-news-election-conspiracy-theories (Accessed: November 2016).

Speri, A. and Biddle, S. (2016) *Facebook removes potential evidence of police brutality too readily, activists say.* Available at: https://theintercept.com/2016/08/08/facebook-removes-potential-evidence-of-police-brutality-too-readily-activists-say/ (Accessed: October 2016).

Stark, L. and Crawford, K. (2015) 'The conservatism of Emoji: Work, affect, and communication', *Social Media + Society*, 1(2). doi: 10.1177/2056305115604853.

Steinmetz, K. (2014) *Teen girls describe the harsh unspoken rules of online popularity.* Available at: http://time.com/3067694/weheartit-teen-girls-bullying-instagram/ (Accessed: August 2016).

Stepanikova, I., Nie, N.H. and He, X. (2010) 'Time on the Internet at home, loneliness, and life satisfaction: Evidence from panel time-diary data', *Computers in Human Behavior*, 26(3), pp. 329–338. doi: 10.1016/j.chb.2009.11.002.

Stone, A.A. and Brownell, K.D. (1994) 'The stress-eating paradox: Multiple daily measurements in adult males and females', *Psychology & Health*, 9(6), pp. 425–436. doi: 10.1080/08870449408407469.

Sumner, M. (2016) *Someone is lying about electric cars on the internet.* Available at: http://www.dailykos.com/story/2016/5/6/1524012/-Someone-is-lying-about-electric-cars-on-the-internet (Accessed: August 2016).

Surowiecki, J. (2016) *What Happened To The Ice Bucket Challenge?* Available at: http://www.newyorker.com/magazine/2016/07/25/als-and-the-ice-bucket-challenge (Accessed: July 2016).

Tait, A. (2016) *'I was frozen to the spot': The psychological dangers of autoplay video.* Available at: http://www.newstatesman.com/science-tech/internet/2016/08/i-was-frozen-spot-psychological-dangers-autoplay-video (Accessed: August 2016).

Taylor, A. and Sadowski, J. (2015) *How companies turn your Facebook activity into a credit score.* Available at: https://www.thenation.com/article/

how-companies-turn-your-facebook-activity-credit-score/ (Accessed: 2 August 2016).

Thomson, I. (2016) *Facebook 'glitch' that deleted the Philando Castile shooting vid: It was the police – sources*. Available at: http://www.theregister. co.uk/2016/07/08/castile_shooting_police_deletion/ (Accessed: 10 July 2016).

Toor, A. (2016) *Facebook begins tracking non-users around the internet*. Available at: http://www.theverge.com/2016/5/27/11795248/facebook-ad-network-non-users-cookies-plug-ins (Accessed: September 2016).

Torres, S.J. and Nowson, C.A. (2007) 'Relationship between stress, eating behavior, and obesity', *Nutrition*, 23(11-12), pp. 887–894. doi: 10.1016/j. nut.2007.08.008.

Troisi, J.D. and Gabriel, S. (2011) 'Chicken soup really is good for the soul: "Comfort food" fulfills the need to belong', *Psychological Science*, 22(6), pp. 747–753. doi: 10.1177/0956797611407931.

Turkle, S. (2011) *Alone together: Why we expect more from technology and less from each other*. New York: Basic Books.

Wagner, A. (2014) *The sun just keeps getting it wrong on human rights – Adam Wagner*. Available at: https://inforrm.wordpress.com/2014/08/06/ the-sun-just-keeps-getting-it-wrong-on-human-rights-adam-wagner/ (Accessed: June 2015).

Wagner, D.D., Altman, M., Boswell, R.G., Kelley, W.M. and Heatherton, T.F. (2013) 'Self-regulatory depletion enhances neural responses to rewards and Impairs top-down control', *Psychological Science*, 24(11), pp. 2262–2271. doi: 10.1177/ 0956797613492985.

Wajcman, J. (2015) *Pressed forTtime: The Acceleration of Life in Digital Capitalism*. United States: University of Chicago Press.

Wang, J.-L., Gaskin, J., Wang, H.-Z. and Liu, D. (2016) 'Life satisfaction moderates the associations between motives and excessive social networking site usage', *Addiction Research & Theory*, pp. 1–8. doi: 10.3109/16066359.2016.1160283.

Wang, J.-L., Wang, H.-Z., Gaskin, J. and Wang, L.-H. (2015) 'The role of stress and motivation in problematic smartphone use among college students', *Computers in Human Behavior*, 53, pp. 181–188. doi: 10.1016/j. chb.2015.07.005.

Warner, M. (2015) *Learning my lesson*. Available at: http://www.lrb.co.uk/v37/ n06/marina-warner/learning-my-lesson (Accessed: September 2016).

Waxman, O.B. (2014) *People called the police because Facebook went down*. Available at: http://time.com/3071049/facebook-down-police/ (Accessed: October 2015).

We Are Social (2008) *Digital in 2016 - we are social Singapore*. Available at: http://wearesocial.com/sg/special-reports/digital-2016 (Accessed: July 2016).

Webb, W. (2016) *Facebook and Israel officially announce collaboration to censor social media content*. Available at: http://www.renegade tribune. com/facebook-israel-officially-announce-collaboration-censor-social media-content/ (Accessed: September 2016).

Webster, S.C. (2012) *Low-wage Facebook contractor leaks secret censorship list*. Available at: http://www.rawstory.com/2012/02/low-wage-facebook-contractor-leaks-secret-censorship-list/ (Accessed: July 2016).

Wenzel, M., Kubiak, T. and Conner, T.S. (2016) 'Self-control in daily life: How affect may boost or sabotage efforts at self-control', *Social Psychological and Personality Science*, 7(3), pp. 195–203. doi: 10.1177/1948550616632578.

West, A.N. (2016) *The Aesthetics of Degradation*. London: Repeater Books.

Wiederhold, B.K. (2012) 'As parents invade Facebook, teens Tweet more', *Cyberpsychology, Behavior, and Social Networking*, 15(8), pp. 385–385. doi: 10.1089/cyber.2012.1554.

Wilson, G. (2015) *Your Brain on Porn: Internet Pornography and the Emerging Science of Addiction*. United Kingdom: Commonwealth Publishing.

Wong, D. (2015) *Report: Social media drove 31.24% of overall visits to sites*. Available at: https://blog.shareaholic.com/social media-traffic-trends-01-2015/ (Accessed: September 2016).

Wong, J.C. (2016) *Mark Zuckerberg accused of abusing power after Facebook deletes 'napalm girl' post*. Available at: https://www.theguardian.com/technology/2016/sep/08/facebook-mark-zuckerberg-napalm-girl-photo-vietnam-war (Accessed: September 2016).

Wood, R.T.A. (2007) 'Problems with the concept of video game "Addiction": Some case study examples', *International Journal of Mental Health and Addiction*, 6(2), pp. 169–178. doi: 10.1007/s11469-007-9118-0.

Woods, B. (2016) *Facebook deactivated Korryn Gaines' account during standoff, police say*. Available at: https://www.theguardian.com/us-news/2016/aug/03/korryn-gaines-facebook-account-baltimore-police (Accessed: August 2016).

World Economic Forum (2016) *Digital Wildfires in a Hyperconnected world*. Available at: http://reports.weforum.org/global-risks-2013/risk-case-1/digital-wildfires-in-a-hyperconnected-world/ (Accessed: October 2016).

Yalom, M. (1997) *A History of the Breast*. New York: Ballantine Books.

Zuboff, S. (2016) *Google as a fortune teller: The secrets of surveillance capitalism*. Available at: http://www.faz.net/aktuell/feuilleton/debatten/the-digital-debate/shoshana-zuboff-secrets-of-surveillance-capitalism-14103616. html (Accessed: May 2016).

Zuckerberg, M. (2016) *A lot of you have asked what we're doing..* Available at: https://www.facebook.com/zuck/posts/ 10103269806149061 (Accessed: November 2016).

Zuckerman, E. (2008) *The Cute Cat Theory of Digital Activism - talk at ETech.* Available at: http://www.ethanzuckerman.com/blog/2008/ 03/08/the-cute-cat-theory-talk-at-etech/ (Accessed: March 2012).

Zuckerman, M. (1980) *Sensation Seeking: Beyond the Optimal Level of Arousal.* New York: Halsted Press Division of Wiley.

Acknowledgements

Thanks first to **Tariq Goddard**, my publisher for this project, who took very little time or convincing to see the same potential that I saw in the book proposal I submitted to Repeater (and which I later found to contain several embarrassing typos that he had graciously looked past). The entire team at Repeater Books, who have guided this book very smoothly through its various stages, also have my profound thanks.

I thank my colleagues at City, University of London for starting me on the journey that would lead me to the issues in this book, and my colleagues at the University of the West of England for providing me with an engaged, supportive and collegiate environment in which to finish the book.

I also thank the staff at the libraries of City, University of London, Goldsmiths, University of London and especially the Bower Ashton campus of the University of the West of England, where I wrote much of this book, for their assistance and hard work.

Warm thanks to my students over the years at every institution where I have taught, for pushing me, teaching me, and being so willing to consider new ideas.

Thanks to all the researchers, bloggers, journalists, writers and academics referenced in this book or appearing in the bibliography (except for the *Daily Mail* and the Murdoch press, which were mostly used when no other source was available).

I would like to acknowledge the firm support of **Bev Skeggs** and the trustees of the Sociological Review Foundation charity in providing gainful, flexible employment during my work on this book, and I also want to thank the clients of my company VSC Creative for their support and patience.

Thanks also to the staff and residents of the **Pervasive Media Studio** at Watershed, Bristol, for providing a convivial and supportive working environment.

If I can write at all, it is largely due to the excellent English teachers I had at state schools up until the age of eighteen. Many thanks to all of them for their accommodating and persistent instruction.

Most importantly, the opportunity to write this book, as well as to think about and develop what became the arguments within it, would never have happened without the varied contributions of quite a few very special people whom I am extremely lucky to know:

Heartfelt thanks must go first of all to my friends and comrades **Alex Wood, Victoria Bogdan-Tejeda, Jack Latham, Joël Vacheron, Manny Castro, Nat Broekman, Matt Rubin Berger, Vanessa Raymond, Leah Bowden, Marcus Hemsley, Alina Papp, Melody Donoso, Yasmeen Narayan, Dana Seman, Alexis Karlin, Kathrine Anker, Jaime Concha, Valeria Dessì, Nell Osborne, Jeremy Evans, Pavel Miller, Ken Danquah, Jack Aldwinckle, Chris Seigal, Douglas Ackerman, Stephanie Söhnchen, Michael Barton-Sweeney, Belayet Hosain, Chris Brauer, Jenn Barth, Jill Lewis, Ruthie Wilson Gilmore, Craig Gilmore, Emma Uprichard, Anthony Barnett, Les Back, Ed Vulliamy, Isaac Julien, Mark Nash, Antoine Zacharias, Christine Zacharias, Maggie Weber, Andrew Dade** and **Shauna Dade** for generous support, interest, hospitality, and emailing of relevant links.

Special thanks to **Rebecca Lewis-Smith, Simone Zacharias, Tábata Mazzochin** and **Ella Reed** — diligent and caring long-term friends whose belief in me and unconditional acceptance of who I am, even when they have found me at my worst, has emboldened and strengthened me greatly. They also read drafts and provided much-needed feedback.

I met and worked with **Emanuelle Degli Esposti** as a very capable journalist and editor, but we quickly became friends. It was deep in conversation with Emanuelle in early 2013 that the idea of "filling" a "void" came to us in reference to the themes that later became this book. It was our idea; thanks for letting me run with it.

Likewise, I would never have been so well equipped to make a serious consideration of social media or understand their significance were it not for the many things I learned from my friend **Maz Hardey**, who also made some important suggestions as this book developed.

My friend **Adam E. Smith** has been extremely supportive of this project throughout, and was the first person to provide feedback on any draft, in which he was gentle but firm.

Eddie Tejeda, who I first met as a 19 year-old who had a web server under his desk, one floor above my dorm room, during my first week at Hampshire College, has been one of my closest friends ever since. He taught me to code and introduced me to GNU/Linux, Apache HTTP Server, the Free Software movement, hacking, and the infrastructure of the internet. His encouragement, friendship and contribution to this book have been enormous.

Fellow bass player and longtime friend **Thomas Zacharias** has not only always been there when it mattered, he has also been a fan of this project since it was just an idea. Not only did he "get" it as soon as I mentioned it, cautiously one October evening in 2014, but the PhD proposal he insisted I write to finish the project became the proposal I submitted to Repeater for this book. I can never thank him enough for his encouragement and intellectual guidance, and I hope that in shortcutting straight to a book without submitting to the additional rigour of a PhD, I have still done justice to the potential that he saw.

My other "brother from another mother" **Phil Bowden**, although far away in California, has always provided the truth when I need to hear it. Not only has he been a true comrade, he has taught me more than I could ever quantify about numerous subjects from critical philosophy to the pursuit of musical virtuosity to not losing hope in the future. His generous willingness to read draft after draft of this book and to Skype for hours to discuss this work has also been appreciated more than I can express.

Lucia Trimbur not only provided invaluable feedback on early drafts of one of the more challenging chapters of this book, being a published author herself; she has been a uniquely important and supportive friend before and during this process. Despite often being thousands of miles away, she has always been close.

Mandy Rose has been there not only as a close family friend who I could talk to unendingly about our shared interests in media and culture (and a great range of other topics), but as a media pioneer in her own right who was one of the first to show me that there were important intellectual questions to be explored in the digital world. Her generosity and hospitality have also been much appreciated.

Extra special love and appreciation go to **Eleanor Weber-Ballard** for her sage advice, steadfast encouragement, helpful ideas and fantastic company. I'm not sure I'd have truly believed I could complete this book, were it not for her.

Finally, there's some family to shout out. **Fran Ware, Cath Richins, Honor Ware, Eleanor Ware, Elizabeth Ware, Caroline Ware, Darla Jane Gilroy, Matthew Gilroy, Simon McBurney** and **Cassie Yukawa-McBurney** are the most supportive and hospitable extended family I could wish for.

Very late one night when I was about four and a half, my peaceful sleep was disturbed by the extremely vigorous and healthy first cries of a newborn baby. Shortly thereafter, I was introduced to the amazing sister I'd always wanted. Speaking not as an older brother but as an equal, it will always be my amazing good fortune to have as my only sibling a human being so extraordinarily kind, intelligent and creative as **Cora**. Our conversations about the world have contributed immeasurably to this project.

Lastly but most of all, I thank my parents. I have always been inspired by their intellectual command of the world around them and their tireless, passionate, but calm determination to make that world a better place. There is a lot that I could say here, but above all I thank them for their infinite support and generosity, and for inspiring me, every day, to try to be both an effective troublemaker and a decent, unconditionally compassionate human being.

Index

Repeater Books

is dedicated to the creation of a new reality. The landscape of twenty-first-century arts and letters is faded and inert, riven by fashionable cynicism, egotistical self-reference and a nostalgia for the recent past. Repeater intends to add its voice to those movements that wish to enter history and assert control over its currents, gathering together scattered and isolated voices with those who have already called for an escape from Capitalist Realism. Our desire is to publish in every sphere and genre, combining vigorous dissent and a pragmatic willingness to succeed where messianic abstraction and quiescent co-option have stalled: abstention is not an option: we are alive and we don't agree.